Twayne's United States Authors Series

Sylvia E. Bowman, *Editor*

INDIANA UNIVERSITY

Orestes A. Brownson

ORESTES A. BROWNSON

by AMERICO D. LAPATI
Mt. St. Rita Novitiate

Twayne Publishers, Inc. :: New York

MANUFACTURED IN THE UNITED STATES OF AMERICA BY
UNITED PRINTING SERVICES, INC.
NEW HAVEN, CONN.

To My Parents

Preface

ORESTES BROWNSON has been classified by Theodore Maynard as "the most remarkable mind American Catholicism has produced,"[1] and by Lord Acton as the most penetrating thinker of his day in America.[2] Brownson's life spanned the nineteenth century; he wrote extensively about the main religious, political, and social issues of his era. But if one delves into any anthology of American authors, even of Catholic anthologies, Brownson receives mere passing mention; only a few offer even an excerpt from an essay of this brilliant journalist.

The present study seeks a higher niche for Brownson in American letters, if the author is studied objectively and dispassionately. The need exists to demonstrate that Brownson viewed the problems of his day with such forcefulness and insight that to neglect his assessments of nineteenth-century thought is to ignore one of the country's greatest minds. It is not the purpose of this study to ask the reader to agree with all or even a part of what Brownson wrote; rather, it is to request respect for the views of a journalist whose dedication to truth as he saw it outweighed any desire for popularity, acclaim, or worldly advantage.

That Brownson has not been widely read and studied is not surprising. His *Works*, edited by his son Henry, have long been out of print; and their format is such that it hardly invites the reader to a thorough study of the author's essays. Furthermore, the author's too frequent change of religious affiliation and of social and political views led to his being dubbed a "weathervane." He did not seek to please his readers by championing popular causes. He preferred to stand alone in the pursuit of truth, come what may. Van Wyck Brooks has put the case succinctly in his analysis of why Brownson could not rally a steadfast following behind him: "he was too Yankee for the Catholics and too Catholic for the Yankees."[3]

More recent studies of Brownson, now that the storm in which he wrote has subsided, have urged a reappraisal of his thought. Schlesinger hopes that "an age more sympathetic with men who would not compromise and would not retreat will accord him his rightful place. He is part of the national heritage."[4] Kirk has expressed the belief that "in the latter half of the twentieth century, more attention may be paid to Brownson than he received in the past hundred years."[5]

To aid in the hoped-for reappraisal of Brownson in the twentieth century this study aims primarily to serve as an introduction to his life and thought. Attempting to read the collected *Works* amounts to a herculean task for the novice in the study of Brownson. Even the scholarly works of Schlesinger and Maynard offer obstacles for a penetration of the main outline of Brownson's life and thought. Accordingly, as a primer, this work divides itself into the main facets of the author's life and thought: religious, socio-economic, political, and literary criticism. Such a plan introduces the reader to a delineated, yet integrated, résumé of Brownson in the different fields in which he wrote and contributed to the thought of the nineteenth century.

In introducing Brownson to the student and general reader, I have placed emphasis upon the writings and those events in the author's life that occasioned them; for writing was the author's life—of over fifty years of continuously setting forth religious, socio-economic, and political views. The adopted method does admit some repetition of events and writings but is, nevertheless, free of the complicated details of a strictly chronological presentation; and it does prepare the student for the more profound studies of Schlesinger and Maynard, whose works follow the chronological plan of Brownson's life and thought.

Few, if any, persons can be expected to agree with all of Brownson's views. But possibly the twentieth century can help exonerate the nineteenth century's bias by a more objective and dispassionate appraisal of one of America's most controversial, yet most stimulating, thinkers.

Grateful acknowledgment is made to the Very Rev. Mariner T. Smith, O.P., J.C.D., S.T.M., Professor of Canon Law, Dominican House of Studies, Washington, D.C., and to Paul Van K. Thomson, Ph.D., Professor of English, Providence College, Providence, R.I., for their reading of the manuscript and for their valuable suggestions and criticisms.

AMERICO D. LAPATI

Cumberland, Rhode Island
October, 1964

Contents

Chronology

1803   Orestes Brownson born in Stockbridge, Vermont, September 16, son of Sylvester Augustus Brownson and Relief Metcalf.

1809   Father died; Orestes placed under care of elderly couple on a small farm in Royalton, Vermont.

1817   Brought to Ballston Spa, in upstate New York, to live with mother, twin sister, and two elder brothers. Had a brief stay at a neighboring academy, but left to work in a printer's office.

1822   Joined Presbyterian Church at Ballston Spa.

1823   Taught school in Stillwater in upstate New York.

1824   Taught school in Detroit, Michigan. Became a Universalist.

1825   Taught school in Elbridge, New York.

1826   Ordained a Universalist preacher at Jaffrey, New Hampshire.

1827   Married Sally Healy (a former pupil) of Elbridge, New York.

1828   First son, Orestes A., Jr., born.

1829   Editor of Universalist journal, *Gospel Advocate and Impartial Investigator*. Corresponding editor of *Free Enquirer*, periodical of Robert Owen and Fanny Wright. Editor of Genesee *Republican and Herald of Reform*, published at Leroy, New York. Son, John Healy, born.

1830   Left Universalists; became a skeptic in religious matters.

1831   An Independent preacher.

1832   Became a Unitarian preacher at Walpole, New Hampshire. Edited and published *The Philanthropist*.

1834   Unitarian preacher at Canton, Massachusetts. Wrote *Charles Elwood*, a fictional account of his skepticism, but not published until 1840. Third son, William Ignatius, born.

1835   Fourth son, Henry Francis, born.

1836   Began to hold independent services in Boston for the Society for Christian Union and Progress. Continued until 1844. Published his first book, *New Views of Christianity, Society, and the Church*. Editor of weekly journal, *Boston Reformer*.

1838   Established *Boston Quarterly Review*. Appointed steward of United States Marine Hospital at Chelsea, Massachusetts, as a reward for supporting Van Buren for President.

1839   First daughter, Sarah Nicolena, born.

1840   Wrote articles on "Laboring Classes" to aid Van Buren and the Democratic Party in the presidential election. Lost faith in the people as their own rulers and began to tend toward conservatism in religion, politics, and economics. Another son, George, born.

1842   At Brook Farm, West Roxbury, Massachusetts. Wrote *Mediatorial Life of Jesus*. Wrote for periodical, *Democratic Review*.

1843   Wrote series on "Mission of Jesus" for *The Christian World*. A son, Edward Patrick, born.

1844   Converted to Roman Catholicism. Founded *Brownson's Quarterly Review* in Boston.

1845   Last and eighth child, Charles Joseph Maria, born.

1849   Received letter of encouragement and approval from American bishops for articles in defense of Roman Catholicism; but later articles on nativism, parochial schools, social and political topics began to lead him into conflict with co-religionists and hierarchy. Son, George, died.

1851   Objected to friendly reception given by American press and political leaders to Louis Kossuth, Hungarian revolutionary. Son, Charles Joseph Maria, died.

1853   Campaigned successfully against changing Massachusetts State Constitution by simple majority vote.

1854   Wrote novel, *The Spirit-Rapper: an Autobiography*.

1855 Left Boston for New York.

1856 Archbishop Hughes of New York publicly criticized Brownson.

1857 Moved to Elizabeth, New Jersey. Wrote autobiography, *The Convert: or Leaves from My Experience.*

1858 Son, John Healy, died.

1860 Denounced to Prefect of the Congregation of the Propaganda of the Faith in Rome for articles on the relationship between spiritual and temporal powers.

1862 Unsuccessful Republican candidate for Congress in third district of New Jersey.

1864 Worked unsuccessfully against President Lincoln's renomination. Withdrew publication of *Quarterly Review.* His son, William Ignatius, an officer in Union army, accidentally killed; Edward Patrick also killed in action at Reams' Station, Virginia.

1865 Wrote *The American Republic.*

1866- Contributed to newly founded periodicals, *Ave Maria*
1873 and *The Catholic World.*

1872 Wife died.

1873 Resumed publication of *Quarterly Review* and published until fall of 1875.

1875 Visited son Henry in Detroit.

1876 Died on April 17.

Orestes A. Brownson

CHAPTER 1

The Searcher for Religious Truth

AMERICA in the first half of the nineteenth century was in a period of intellectual and reform ferment; and in this period of profound changes Orestes Brownson was born. Influenced by the more radical approaches to reform, he formulated his early views on religion, society, and politics. But further reflection and experience led him to modify his earlier views. Therefore, to limn the period in which he lived requires—for a proper view of him—an analysis of the historical setting.

The great American dream of equal opportunity and justice for all in a democracy had not yet been realized. The Industrial Revolution had divided society into the privileged capitalists and the downtrodden laborers. "Thus far," wrote Stephen Simpson, a leader in the Philadelphia Workingmen's Party, "we perceive our constitution of *equal rights* to be the merest untenanted skeleton of liberty that the imagination of man can conceive; which, by its *operation,* creates aristocracy, privileges, extortion, monopoly, and overgrown fortunes, and which, by its *letter,* declares that equality of rights shall be guaranteed to all and the pursuit of happiness to be a common boon secured to industry by the equity of her principles and the simplicity of her laws."[1]

The "have-nots" in American society were not, however, without sympathizers. Intellectuals, writers, and clergymen proposed theories and programs of reform. Hardly an area of man's life was left untouched. The range of varied suggestions ran the gamut of withdrawing peacefully from society and establishing communities free of class rivalry to the changing of the *status quo* by strong, concerted political action. Truly, "the bourgeoning of reformism in the 1830's and 1840's was the most remarkable phenomenon in the social history of that generation."[2]

Contributing basically to the desire for social reform and serving as a stimulation for reform was the change in religious thinking. More liberal Unitarians started a transformation of Christian thought. Unlike the Deists, who looked upon human reason as the source of knowledge of God, nature, and man, the liberal Unitarians continued their belief in revelation and miracles. But it was no longer a Trinitarian concept of God that the liberal Unitarians held: Christ was not a divine person but a great human religious leader. The sternness of Calvinism, once dominant in American religious thought, was dropped. Men were to look to a kind and warmhearted God instead of to an angry, vindictive God. Nor was man the victim of predestination—to be numbered among either the elect or the damned; man was free to work out his own salvation. Providing a practical application to man's life in society, this new liberal trend in theology offered hope and inspiration for social reform. Emphasis was placed on preaching a social gospel in which Christ was viewed as a great humanitarian and ethical leader. Every social evil became the target of reform: lack of free educational institutions, prison conditions, slavery, poor working conditions, mistreatment of orphans and the poor. Even the temperance movement and the women's rights movement began at this point in American history.

As powerful a force as was Unitarianism in liberal religious thought and social humanitarianism at the beginning of the nineteenth century, its sectarian character served as a drawback to its assumption of leadership among the many Christian denominations in the United States. An intellectual movement known as Transcendentalism, nonsectarian in its religious character, was in a better position to assume leadership.

Transcendentalism received its inspiration from a variety of sources, principally from such British Romanticists as Coleridge and from such German philosophical idealists as Kant. Transcendentalism was based on a belief in the innate divinity of every man and his ability through intuition, which transcends pure reason, to understand God. Biblical revelation and church-formulated creeds were not required. Knowledge of God, according to Transcendentalism, was possible to the individual who would listen to the voice within himself. This American philosophical idealism rejected the absolutistic and nationalistic tendencies of German idealism, especially as exemplified by Hegel, with its emphasis upon the individualistic character of man's spiritual nature. The human spirit transcended the material and lower aspects of physical nature. Unlike materialistic naturalism, Transcendentalism stressed man's spirit in contrast to his body.

When Transcendentalism viewed society as in need of reform, it insisted that reform should be aimed at spiritual freedom and self-realization. The Enlightenment rationalists sought reform through material self-improvement. Transcendentalism considered materialism and its consequent absorption in making gains from industry and commerce as evil. Man's spiritual nature —intellectual, moral, and religious—transcended material experience. Man would attain perfectibility of his spiritual nature through intuition, insight, and poetic vision rather than through factual knowledge.

Transcendentalism numbered among its exponents at one time or another many American writers of the 1830's and the 1840's, among whom were Ralph Waldo Emerson, Theodore Parker, Bronson Alcott, William Ellery Channing, Henry Thoreau, Margaret Fuller, George Bancroft, and Orestes Brownson. They expressed their views, frequently divergent, in a little magazine called the *Dial*.

To aid the free cultivation of man's spiritual nature, many Transcendentalists escaped from the materialistic competition of city life and sought refuge in "back to nature" communities. Most notable of these utopian experiments that were in varying degrees socialistic was the community founded by George Ripley at West Roxbury, Massachusetts, and known as Brook Farm. As a cooperative enterprise, Brook Farm attempted in the words of its founder Ripley

> to insure a more natural union between intellectual and manual labor than now exists; to combine the thinker and the worker, as far as possible in the same individual; to guarantee the highest mental freedom, by providing all with labor adapted to their tastes and talents, and securing to them the fruits of their industry; to do away with the necessity of menial services by opening the benefits of education and the profits of labor to all; and thus to prepare a society of liberal, intelligent, and cultivated persons, whose relations with each other would permit a wholesome and simple life that can be led amidst the pressure of our competitive institutions.[3]

Brook Farm's members, in its six-year history, willingly tried to serve as missionaries for the cause of socialism through their writings and lectures.

But Brook Farm was not the only American socialist experiment in the generation before the Civil War. German pietists, under the leadership of George Rapp, formed a number of socialist communities in several states. John Humphrey Noyes founded the Oneida community, near Seneca Lake, New York. Adin Ballou founded the Hopedale community near Milford, Massachusetts. The Mormons Joseph Smith and Brigham Young organized socialist communities. These socialist utopias were of religious origin and demonstrated an optimistic faith in the perfectibility of human institutions. Their hope was to offer in their experiment a model for a new and better social order inspired by the Christian Gospel. More than fifty similar experiments can be numbered in nineteenth-century America.[4]

Utopian socialism, however, was also of non-religious inspiration. Most notable of these experiments was the one at New Harmony, Indiana, founded by Robert Owen, who had come to the United States from England and Scotland in 1824. The members of this community were asked to undergo a transformation from the selfish habits of the old order of competitive industrial society to the communitarian interests of the new socialist order. But the strong individualistic tendencies of Americans created or encouraged obstinate adherence to self-interest and social distinctions, thus rendering ineffective the ideal of harmonious views and needs in a society that was to be a common family.

Motivated by the same humanitarian and socialistic thinking of Robert Owen, Frances Wright, daughter of a Scottish tradesman, established a community for Negroes in Nashoba, Tennessee. In this experiment Negro slaves would work in a common effort to acquire skills enabling them to earn a livelihood when they became free. But lack of leadership led to bankruptcy and Wright's views on Christian morality and miscegenation won no sympathizers to her venture. She later devoted her energies to the cause of the workingman and became editor of the *Free Enquirer*, to which Orestes Brownson made contributions for a brief time.

Two French socialists, Charles Fourier and Étienne Cabet, influenced the establishment of utopian communities in the United

States in the generation preceding the Civil War. Albert Brisbane, a student of Fourier in Paris, in cooperation with Horace Greeley, founded a Fourierist colony near Red Bank, New Jersey. Cabet and his followers organized socialist communities in several American states from the 1840's to the 1860's. These utopias proved ineffective and ended in failure. Fourierism, however, did gain some followers at the short-lived Brook Farm experiment and caused a few changes in the Transcendentalist community.

But peaceful withdrawal was not seen as the sole solution to the inequities brought about by industrialization. Americans could well learn from the struggle that was taking place in England in the first half of the nineteenth century. The English working class reacted to the *laissez-faire* economic philosophy of Adam Smith. The deplorable working conditions and treatment of workers provided data to support the socialistic theses of Friedrich Engels' *Condition of the Working Class in 1844* and of Karl Marx's *Das Kapital*. Economic discontent led laborers to seek to better their lot by political agitation, from which arose the Chartist movement in 1838. Although the British government remained adamant about not granting concessions to the Chartists after a full decade of agitation, the movement focused attention on the plight of the workingman at the hands of the industrial capitalists and paved the way for reform in the latter half of the nineteenth century. Sympathizers from all segments of British society joined in protest against economic liberalism: clergymen initiated a social gospel movement which branded the degradation of the working classes as unchristian; humanitarian factory owners, like Robert Owen, began reforms in their own mills and sought without success effective legislation from Parliament; political leaders, most notably Benjamin Disraeli, regarded improvement in the social and economic conditions of the lower classes as a means of strengthening the country. The demands of the working class, once regarded as radical, were later hailed as signs of democratic progress.

Repercussions of the Chartist movement were also felt in the United States, for workingmen saw in labor organizations a means to improve their lot. Workers were encouraged by the election in 1828 of Andrew Jackson, whom they regarded as a "son of the soil" and as a "man of the people." Jacksonian democracy led to the extension of suffrage by removing the property qualification for voting and to an increased popular participation in politics. With more workers having the right to vote, they could achieve greater gains through their political activities. Theophilus Fisk, a Universalist minister in New England, urged the workers to "teach the lawgivers a salutary lesson at the polls . . .; vote for no man who is not pledged to maintain your cause at all risks and at every hazard. If you are united, your strength is well nigh omnipotent."[5]

Hundreds of local trade societies were formed from 1825 to 1837. Workingmen's parties were formed in almost all industrial cities. The Democratic Party of Andrew Jackson, however, provided workingmen a focus in national politics. "From Maine to Georgia," one newspaper reported in 1830, "within a few months past, we discern symptoms of a revolution, which will be second to none save that of '76."[6] Another newspaper observed that "throughout this vast republic the farmers, mechanics and workingmen are assembling . . . to impart to its laws and administration those principles of liberty and equality unfolded in the Declaration of our Independence."[7]

The depression that followed the panic of 1837, however, dealt a severe blow to the growth and strength of American labor organizations. Losses in membership and funds due to extensive unemployment rendered labor unions ineffective. With no basis for collective bargaining, the workers were left at the mercy of their employers—a situation that was to exist until the post-Civil War period.

In this context of intellectual and reform ferment, Brownson was born and grew up. At first he was enchanted by many of the ideas and leaders of his era, but, upon more sobering reflection, he disavowed himself from its more radical tendencies.

I Calvinist Background

Orestes Augustus Brownson was born on September 16, 1803, in the town of Stockbridge, Windsor County, Vermont. His father Sylvester was a native of Hartford County, Connecticut, and his mother, Relief Metcalf, of Keene, New Hampshire. The Brownsons had come to Stockbridge, a frontier town of about a hundred inhabitants, shortly after their marriage. Orestes and his twin sister, Daphne Augusta, were the youngest of the six children in the family.

Two years after Orestes' birth his father died. Despite efforts of his mother to keep the family together, it was decided that Orestes, then six years old, be placed under the care of an elderly couple steeped in New England Congregationalism, in the neighboring town of Royalton, Vermont. Hard-working, plain country people, they tilled the soil for a livelihood. Although the couple belonged to no particular religious denomination and did not attend any religious meetings, they brought up Orestes in a religious environment of God-fearing and moral honesty and uprightness that became the foundation of his later search for religious truth. In typical Calvinist mold, Brownson's childhood was characterized by a stern and severe Puritan morality that envisioned disobedience to parental authority as liable to the vengeful curse of God. Plentiful reading of religious works took up his childhood days rather than the playing of games, since other children of his age were not readily available in the neighborhood. Brownson remembered having read through the entire Bible by the time he reached eight years of age, and he knew by heart a great part of it by the time he was fourteen. Watts's *Psalms* and *Divine Songs, The Franklin Primer,* Davis' *Sermons,* and Edward's *History of the Redemption* were the few other religious books in the couple's meager library, which Brownson recalled having read. Deprived of youthful companionship and constantly under the surveillance of old people, Brownson reminisced in later life, "Properly speaking I had no childhood."[8]

As the elderly couple with whom he lived attended no church meetings, Brownson was not a member of any particular denomination. He remembered a strong belief in the Apostle's Creed, without attaching any meaning to the articles in the Creed affirming faith in the "Holy Catholic Church" and "the Communion of the Saints." In attempts to satisfy his religious tendencies Brownson on his own attended the meetings of the Methodists and Christians, a sect founded in New England by Elias Smith and Abner Jones; moreover, their meetings were more readily accessible to him than the other Protestant denominations in the town. Although he was told that these two groups differed in their beliefs, the only difference he noted was that the Methodist preachers had stronger lungs and gave more vivid pictures of the sufferings of the damned in hell.[9] Both groups, however, convinced him that he must either be born again or go to hell—get religion or be damned. But as yet Brownson did not seek admission into any particular sect.

At the age of fourteen Orestes' mother took him to live with the family at Ballston Spa in upstate New York. A job in a printer's office followed a brief formal education. His own readings in theology and associations with people of varied religious persuasions produced in his mind "a stream that flows out of darkness into darkness."[10] Not a member of any church, he found himself with "no belief to sustain me and no worship to refresh me."[11] A chance attendance at a Presbyterian service convinced Brownson that a guide in religious matters could gain for him much more than his own speculations about religious matters. A consultation with the Presbyterian minister led Brownson to accept revelation rather than his own reasoning for faith.

Preferring some certainty to utter confusion in religious matters, he joined the local Presbyterian church in 1822, a decision he later referred to as "the act of an intellectual desperado."[12] Brownson could not take to the doctrines of the total depravity of human nature and predestination with possible eternal punishment as espoused by Calvinism. He was even asked not to associate with non-members, all to be classified as sinners. He had hoped for an authoritative teacher in religious matters, but when he made this request he was told merely to read the Bible and beg the Holy Spirit for enlightenment. Disclaiming all authority to teach him by an authoritative set of doctrines, except those of total depravity and predestination, the Presbyterians made Brownson feel that he gave up his intellectual freedom in vain and was bound only to an illusory authority.[13] These Calvinist doctrines gave him a morbid outlook and caused him anguish. His diary discloses his reactions: "Now ends another year. Yes, I have sinned every day, every hour, yea, and every breath has been drawn in iniquity: every thought and every imagination of my heart has been evil, only evil, and that continually. . . . How little do I feel religion, how cold, how dead in the service of the Lord! . . . I see nothing in me that looks like religion; I am base; I am corrupt, . . . lost to every sense of religion."[14] Brownson could not take for long what appeared to him as so inhuman a religion; so he left the Presbyterians early in 1824.

II *Universalism*

At the age of twenty in 1823, Brownson began a brief teaching career in Stillwater, another small village near Ballston Spa, New York. Upon casting aside the Presbyterian religion in early 1824, he left New York State for another teaching assignment in Detroit. For a considerable part of 1825, however, he was convalescing from a serious bout with malaria—thus affording him the opportunity to ponder on the future of his soul and the religious doctrines he ought to espouse.

Any religion that taught the antithesis of Calvinism could make a ready appeal to him; and it was in Universalism that this antithesis appeared. For Universalism in contradistinction to Calvinism denied eternal damnation and offered to all men an assurance of salvation. Although Universalists accepted the corroding influence on man's nature of Original Sin, they asserted the hope of salvation through the redemptive work of Christ.

Universalism so appealed to Brownson that he decided to leave a teaching career for one in the ministry. In the autumn of 1826 he formally applied to the Universalist General Convention for the position of preacher in that religious denomination. Having returned to Vermont, he now busied himself in preparation for his new calling and on June 15, 1826, he was ordained a Universalist preacher at Jaffrey, New Hampshire. He subsequently occupied pulpits in Vermont, New Hampshire, and northern New York state, thereby fulfilling his childhood ambition to be a minister.[15] In addition to his preaching he received the appointment of editor of the *Gospel Advocate,* a Universalist semi-monthly journal and the most widely circulated and most influential Universalist periodical. As editor of a theological journal Brownson had a medium to set forth his views and an opportunity to place before his readers a mind in search of religious certainty. Since salvation stood uppermost in his religious aspirations, he had to ascertain beyond doubt the guarantee for its attainability.

Since the doctrine of salvation was contained in the Bible, Brownson applied the test of logic in examining the fount of this belief. He found the texts teaching salvation in Sacred Scripture unable to stand the test of honest criticism; therefore he felt that he could not surrender his reason to the Bible. To command assent, the Bible would have to teach clearly beyond doubt; yet doubt resulted from reading the Bible. He stood puzzled between those who argued salvation and those who argued damnation with equal force based on Scriptural texts. Lacking an authority to assert and interpret the Bible as the undisputed Word of God, Brownson rejected Scripture.[16]

Returning to his own reason, he examined a fundamental tenet of Universalism: its doctrine of punishment. Universalists held that vengeance or vindictive punishment was incompatible with the idea of God Who is all love. All men would, therefore, be saved regardless of their sinful lives because of the abundant mercy of the all-loving God. Brownson could not see unrepented sin go unpunished, and he could not accept Universalism as it made "no objective distinction between virtue and vice, between good and evil." He then even saw in it "the very foundation of morality undermined."[17]

Without a belief in the Scriptures or an authoritative teacher in religious matters, Brownson found himself accepting only the world of the senses. He could neither assert nor deny God's existence, neither believe nor disbelieve in life after death; for both matters were beyond the realm of the senses either to prove or to disprove. Yet his intense desire for some religious belief and love for mankind urged him to draw up what he considered a limited creed before he decided to reject Universalism.

Brownson published in the *Gospel Advocate* the five points of his creed urging every individual to be honest, benevolent and kind to all; to be desirous of procuring the essentials of life for himself and for others; interested in cultivating his mental powers so as to enjoy the goods of the earth and therefore help others do likewise; and to be faithful in upholding these principles, as an indication of service to God and all mankind.[18]

Even though Brownson mentioned God in his creed, his own interpretation of the idea of God was not the God of faith but the God of human reason. His own clarification of this point disclosed that man's end is to be achieved in this life in the possession of earthly goods and happiness, not of God in heaven.[19] He clearly on his own admission was no longer a Christian.

III *Skepticism*

With the rejection of the Scriptures as the revealed word of God, Brownson found himself a skeptic. He began to question the very existence of God, since no logical argument could convince him.[20] He described his intellectual struggle with skepticism in the novel *Charles Elwood, or the Infidel Converted.* He first wrote this work in 1834 but did not publish it until 1840. The book reflects his mind from late 1829 to the beginning of 1831. Although a fictional account, Brownson claimed that "it has been written in earnest spirit for a serious purpose."[21] The characters portrayed are fictitious but the views expressed by Charles Elwood are substantially Brownson's.

"Lost in the wilderness of doubt," a period he regarded as "the winter of my life," Brownson exposed the grounds for his skepticism.[22] He felt that the books of the Bible, having been produced in an unenlightened age, were never open to the criticism that present-day books are. The authors have not undergone the same scrutiny as had outstanding authors of history. The extraordinary feats or miracles set forth in the Bible could not be used to authenticate the Bible, for both profane and sacred writers tend to embellish their views with "miraculous stories."[23] Moreover, miracles are classified as extraordinary simply because they are beyond human comprehension, not necessarily because they are the work of God. To entreaties made to him to believe in God, Charles Elwood merely replied, "If there be a God, perhaps he may one day reveal himself to me also, and I may hope as well as to you."[24]

Arguments for the existence of God are presented to Elwood, but they could not convince a mind always puzzled with the paradox of which came first, the chicken or the egg: "You must first prove that the universe had a beginning before you establish the fact of design. . . . No matter how far you extend the chain of sequences [in reference to the argument from causality], the same problem ever recurs."[25] So Brownson found himself gripped in the coils of skepticism.

It was the death of a loved one that set the infidel of the novel upon a new train of thought. If all life ended in the grave, then he wondered how valuable could the achievements of the present life be? There would be no aim, no end in life: "I existed, but did not live. He who has no future, has no life."[26] This restlessness produced a desperate futility that led him to examine the possibility of immortality. Hope for future betterment of self and of mankind and for the lasting effects of social progress leads man to look beyond the mere present. Thus, the infidel began to see in the efforts toward social equality and love of fellowman a springboard for belief in the Gospel of love as preached by Christ.

A visit to Charles Elwood from an elderly gentleman, a Mr. Howard, "endowed by nature with a warm heart, a clear and discriminating mind," had a most influential effect.[27] Explaining the true purpose of Christianity, Howard was able to win the infidel over to the belief in Christianity; but Elwood still could not see the church and her clergy as "comprehending the real character of Christianity."[28] Neither Catholicism nor Protestantism had preached the truths of Christ as He did, especially in promoting social progress, Elwood felt. But Mr. Howard ably convinced him that Christianity is primarily the poor man's religion, emphasizing his rights, his own lofty nature, his equality before God and hence his capacity for endless progress in truth, love, and goodness.

The strong rationalism believed in by Mr. Elwood could not yet fully let him accept Christianity as a divine institution; for he found that he still could not believe in God. A trip with the congenial Mr. Howard to listen to a sermon by a Mr. Morton became another influential turning point in the infidel's bout with unbelief. But now the presentation of the arguments of God as an intelligent cause responsible for all the workings of nature became convincing. Even as an infidel Charles Elwood could not help being impressed by the strong religious sentiment held by men of all times and places. He further realized his own helplessness and need for a higher power with whom to commune.

With the acceptance of God's existence, Charles Elwood is prepared for belief in the Scriptures as the Word of God. The authors of the sacred books stand apart from other authors. The former are chosen by God to make known to us truths unattainable by the human intellect; the latter merely interpret and make use of the words of God. God Himself commissions sacred writers. Other authors write on their own authority of the views personal to them. So Charles Elwood accepts the argument presented to him: "The prophet is the poet chanting the divine. His soul is full of God and he pours himself out in a stream of harmony on which float along the unsearchable things of God. God moves in him and speaks through him."[29]

Acceptance of the Bible leads to the knowledge of Christ's mission: to found a spiritual kingdom on earth. The nature of this kingdom is not an outward and visible church, but an inward and invisible church. With this explanation by Mr. Morton concerning no need of an external organization, as conceived by Roman Catholicism, Charles Elwood returns to Protestant Christianity. Still somewhat alarmed at the divergent interpretations of Christ's teachings, he nevertheless feels that the essence of the message of Christianity is atonement, man's salvation being made possible through the redemptive work of Christ.

Although he admitted that many good Christians would at first sight be shocked in reading of Charles Elwood's bout with skepticism, the author concluded that the more he examined his doubts the more clear and certain did the truth of Christianity eventually appear to his mind. His faith in Christ became stronger for having doubted.

When Brownson discussed the reactions to his book, he insisted that he wrote the work primarily for the unbeliever, as the unbeliever would be in need of the arguments presented in the book.[30] Contrary to some reviews of his book, Brownson felt that he concentrated on the value of the heart as well as the value of logic in appealing to unbelievers. No man can divest himself of his sentiments and emotions; for, however powerful logic may be, it is utterly insufficient to satisfy the wants of the soul: "All his feelings, all the force of his sentiments, the emotions of the soul are on the side of faith." Love is a "subtler influence" than mere logic.[31]

Brownson also disavowed a former, complete adherence to Benjamin Constant's view of religion as solely a sentiment of the heart. Religion was an idea as well, a conviction by an intelligent being reasoning objectively about his relations to the Creator.[32] Brownson thus regarded both the heart and the mind as necessary in the notion of religion as belief in a Supreme Being.

Upon leaving the Universalists, Brownson became a skeptic in religious matters. He also became involved in the Workingmen's Party movement, with Frances Wright and with the utopian ideas of Robert Owen, for Brownson was desirous of improving man's lot on earth. The reform of society and earthly felicity became his great goals.[33] But he found that these goals could not be achieved without religion, and he constantly found himself reverting to his early religious principles and inclinations. He later wrote of this trying period in his life: "I did not need religion to pull down or destroy society; but the moment I wished to build up, to effect something positive, I found I could not proceed a single step without it. . . . I need, then, religion of some sort as the agent to induce men to make the sacrifices required in the adoption of my plans."[34] Thus Brownson felt that he had to return to his vocation of preacher.

IV *Unitarianism*

In February, 1831, Brownson set himself up as an independent preacher. Although he disclaimed adherence to any Christian sect, he did admit that the views of the Unitarians more nearly approximated the spirit of Christianity than any other sect. As he wrote in *The Philanthropist*, a fortnightly journal which he edited and published,

> Should I assume the name of any party, it should be Unitarian, as that denomination approximates nearer, in my estimation, to the spirit of Christianity than any other. Unitarian discourses are mostly practical; their lessons inculcate charity, a refined moral feeling and universal benevolence . . . but I discover no necessity of assuming any name that can become the rallying point of a sect . . . I am an independent preacher, accountable to my God, to truth, to my country, to the people of my charge, but to no other tribunal.[35]

In 1832, however, he did become a Unitarian minister; for he approved of the Unitarian practice of permitting each preacher to stand on his own convictions rather than to be held to a body of fixed doctrines. During four years as a Unitarian preacher at Walpole, New Hampshire, and at Canton, Massachusetts, Brownson delved into the writings of the French philosophers, most notably Constant, Saint-Simon, Jouffroy, and Cousin. These men envisioned Christianity which gave to the world a gospel of social reform, as having a dynamic force in the social progress of man. Yet to Brownson the Reformation had so rocked Roman Catholicism from its roots that it could no longer be the undisputed leader in promoting Christ's gospel; and Protestantism, with all its divergent sects, was too unorganized to be an effective leader. A new church was needed, free and independent from the dead past and the confused present—the Church of the Future.

In 1836 Brownson published his first book, *New Views of Christianity, Society and the Church*. The occasion for *New Views* was what Brownson regarded as a needed handbook for the Society for Christian Union and Progress in Boston. He had come to Boston at the urging of William Ellery Channing and George Ripley to preach to the laboring classes. These two men felt that Brownson's own experience with skepticism would help in impregnating the laborers with Christian social principles, which they appeared to lack. Brownson saw a tremendous opportunity in this invitation and held religious meetings in Boston's Lyceum Hall. *New Views* became for Brownson a hope for offering a program of social progress based on religion.

The significance of this work is that in it Brownson synthesized the views he had been mulling over in his mind for some time. Christianity was not to be a matter of concern for one day of the week only and for the world to come; rather, it should also be an integral part of man's day-to-day life on earth.

Brownson began his *New Views* by distinguishing between religion and religious institutions. The former is a natural sentiment to man—a universal, permanent, and indestructible desire to honor and worship God; the latter are means which man uses to make possible the expression of his natural sentiment and can vary in different countries and periods of time. Christ in his ministry brought to the world the most perfect religious institution attainable to the human race by joining together sentiment and the institution. But mankind from Christ's contemporaries to the present day has not fully comprehended the profundity of Christ's message and work. The failure of this apprehension is due primarily to misunderstanding the struggle between exces-

sive spiritualism and excessive materialism: spiritualism, by regarding matter as essentially impure and sinful; and materialism,
by regarding as non-existent and imaginary such notions as soul
and heaven. God, moreover, is spirit; and man, essentially matter. Christ, as the God-Man, stands between spirit and matter.
For this role the work of Christ has been described as mediation,
reconciliation, atonement.[36] But the Church emphasized only
that Christ came to redeem spirit from the evil consequences of
its connection with matter and not to atone for both spirit and
matter as separate and distinct entities. In its misapprehension,
the Church made Christ solely a Redeemer, not the Atoner. Having failed to carry on Christ's work to all ages, the Church over-
emphasized spiritualism and became a partisan, not a mediator,
in the struggle between spirit and matter.[37]

Brownson then views all the Church's doctrines and practices
up to the sixteenth century as examples of overemphasizing the
spiritual to the degree that any enjoyment of material goods in
the world would only serve to keep man from attaining salvation. "A dark, silent, friar's frock was the only befitting garb for
nature or for man."[38]

Protestantism arose as a rebellion of the material order against
the spiritual. For the material, however degraded by the Church,
was never annihilated. The material wealth and pleasures
enjoyed by the Papacy itself were in actual practice a contradiction to its long established belief in the supremacy of the
spiritual over the material. The protests of the reformers against
the Church of Rome served to point out the contradiction and
marked a reversal in the history of Christianity from excessive
spiritualism to excessive materialism. Faith then gave way to
reasoning, infallible teaching authority to private interpretation,
the search for spiritual goods to temporal goods, authority to
freedom, and clerical domination to civil and political liberty.[39]

The excessive materialism of Protestantism wore itself out as
the French Revolution was born. What took place in France
under the watchwords of liberty, equality, and fraternity only
demonstrated to what excesses man left without spiritual hopes
and authority can degrade himself: "From that moment enthu-
siasm died, hope in social melioration ceased to be indulged,
and those who had been the most sanguine in their anticipations,
hung down their heads and said nothing; the warmest friends of

humanity apologized for their dreams of liberty and equality; democracy became an accusation, and faith in the perfectibility of mankind a proof of his disordered intellect."[40] Again the pendulum swung to spiritualism as materialism failed to give genuine happiness on earth.

As for spiritualism becoming supreme again, Brownson felt this to be impossible. For man will never divest himself of material interests and aspirations. Man accepts and desires to maintain the material progress that has been made in the social, economic, intellectual, and political spheres. This concept leads Brownson to disclose "our mission": to reconcile spirit and matter, to bring about the atonement—the very mission of Christ. Since Catholicism and Protestantism have not been able to carry out this mission, "This age must realize the atonement, the union of spirit and matter, the destruction of all antagonism and the production of universal peace. God has appointed us to build the new church, the one which shall bring the whole family of man within its sacred enclosure, which shall be able to abide the ravages of time, and against which, 'the gates of hell shall not prevail.' "[41]

The basic truth of the new Church for Brownson is the eventual goodness of man. A penetration of the true meaning of Christ the God-Man is that we are to find divinity in humanity and humanity in divinity. Since God and man are united in one person, both must be holy. The Father and the Son are one; to honor the Son is to honor the Father, humanity as Divinity, man as God. All the material riches of the world are good, as God Himself told us after their creation. With both matter and spirit being real and holy, both are saved; neither is sacrificed but both "coexist as separate elements of the same grand and harmonious whole."[42]

Regarding all God's creation as good will lead to a new civilization in which all political, social, and economic institutions will be remodeled. The gradual achieving of this civilization is making use of God's richest gift to us—the capacity for progress. Man may have begun in weakness and ignorance because God designed him as a progressive being, who can progress only on the condition that he be made less perfect than he may become. The failures of the past should lead man to choose a new direction: "The true priests are those who can quicken in mankind a desire for progress, and urge them forward in the direction of the true, the good, the perfect."[43] Thus man must have a new religion, a religion of progress.

Applying the dialectical technique to historical analysis, Brownson adapted the facts of history to his major propositions. His interpretations of both Roman Catholicism and Protestantism were dialectical exaggerations with facts presented only to support an *a priori* proposition; for neither went to the extremes of spiritualism or materialism. As far as the divinity and the humanity of Christ being misunderstood by the Church, Brownson ignores those heresies in the first several centuries of Christianity which the Church condemned because of their misinterpretation of the true nature of the Incarnation. Still in dread of Calvinism's total depravity of man, Brownson leans toward an impossible perfectibility of human nature.

It is no wonder that *New Views* did not produce the desired effects of persuading adherents to his Church of the future. He noted this fact in an article written for the *Boston Quarterly Review* six years after the publication of his book.[44] Reviewing his own book, Brownson reaffirms its conclusions in the hope that its general design and scope will be better understood. Brownson was not to lose hope in seeing established in the Church of the future his synthesis of Catholicism and Protestantism.

Of greater significance in the development of Brownson's theological thinking is his *The Mediatorial Life of Jesus*. Published as a pamphlet, it was at first a long letter written in June, 1842, to Dr. William Ellery Channing, a fellow Unitarian preacher. In this work Brownson felt that he finally came upon the key that would solve all religious problems: salvation is through Jesus Christ the Mediator.

Brownson begins the letter to Channing by acknowledging him as his "spiritual father," whose writings led him out of doubt to faith in the Bible as God's Word and to Christ as mediator between God and men. He recalls Channing's friendship and the sermon "Likeness to God," so influential in the development of Brownson's religious convictions. Having convinced himself of the role of Christ, he now seeks to offer a method which "reconciles all conflicting theories, discloses new wisdom in that plan [i.e., in the world's salvation], and enables us to take, in its most obvious and literal sense, without any subtlety or refinement, what the Scriptures say of Jesus, and of salvation through his life."[45]

A theological revolution is the true hope of Brownson's method of setting forth Christ as the Mediator. Influenced by the French writer Leroux, whom he described as "a bold champion of social and religious progress," Brownson would extend his views.[46] Leroux feels that the life of the individual and that of the race are inseparably united. Brownson emphasizes that this union is not merely on a human level but also on a spiritual. The life of Christ, human and divine, affects the human race. With a successful presentation of his new method there can be effected "a complete revolution, not in religious belief, but in theological science."[47]

By answering three questions Brownson offers his method: (1) Whence comes the Mediator? (2) What is His work? (3) What is the method by which he performs it? Brownson firmly asserts the divine origin of Jesus in his answer to the first question: "He is from God, who commends his love to us by him."[48] Some religious thinkers regarded Christ solely as human, yet as endowed with more piety and devotion, philanthropy, greater influence on men than most religious leaders. They fail to acknowledge him as a "providential man," sent from God with a mission of salvation to perform. A belief in the Bible as a supernatural book would obviate any such false notion; for there is clearly stated the divine mission of Christ: "For God so loved the world that he gave his only-begotten Son, that those who believe in him may not perish, but may have life everlasting."[49]

Why did God send Christ? In answering this question Brownson takes on a *via media* between the extremes of Calvinism and those who reject altogether the depravity of human nature. He admits his own error in proceeding from one extreme view to the other. Experience, he states, proves unquestionably "an under-current of depravity" in all men, but not to the objectionable point of total depravity. Yet men ought not fall into the error of Transcendentalism which deifies and worships the human soul that they claim "in ourselves are the elements of divinity." It is impossible for man "in any intelligible or legitimate sense of the word, to be *naturally* divine."[50] Relying not solely on experience with human nature but more especially on the teachings of Sacred Scripture, Brownson offers St. Paul's explanation of Original Sin: sin is transmitted from generation to generation through one man, Adam, the moral head of the human race and to whom all mankind is united by inheritance. Brownson continues with St. Paul's explanation that "just as by the disobedience of the one man the many were constituted sinners, so also by the obedience of the one many will be constituted just."[51] The redemption of mankind is the mission of Christ, the new Adam.

How does man receive redemption through Christ as the Mediator? Brownson sets forth this process in a number of propositions. Man cannot commune directly with God and so requires a mediator. This mediator must be of God because God was offended, and yet he must be man because man did the offending. Christ is the God-Man who gives his life not only *for* God but *to* God. Man can have eternal life only in so far as he lives the identical life of Christ.

Basic to all the above propositions is the fact that Christ is Christianity. To reject Christ would be to reject Christianity. Since Christ, moreover, is "the way, the truth, and the life," they who accept Christ as the Mediator share Christ's life. Being the God-Man, they who share his human life also share his divine life. Proceeding to the words of Christ, "He who eats my flesh, and drinks my blood, abides in me and I in him,"[52] Brownson sees the Communion of Christ with all men—men sharing the very life of Christ. This communion, however, is only figurative and not in the Roman Catholic sense of partaking Christ's real body. It is His spirit, not His flesh that communion with Christ provides. In his presentation of Christ's mediatorial life Brownson felt himself more qualified to be a preacher of Christ's Gospel. He still saw no need for a divine commission from any organized Church or for a rite of ordination: "I have God's truth to preach, and I go to preach it not in my own name, nor in the name of any man, nor any set of men, but on the authority of God's Word."[53]

Whatever theological revolution Brownson hoped would result from this new method of setting forth Christ as the Mediator occurred in his own thinking rather than in that of others. In reply to this letter Channing congratulated Brownson on his newly found peace and confidence, but he chided him by commenting: "God made you for something better than to scatter random shot, although these shot may sometimes be grand ideas and hit old errors between wind and water."[54] Emerson more bluntly summarized his reactions by labeling the method as "all positive, local and idolatrous."[55]

But for Brownson a theological revolution was in full gear. His views set him apart from his fellow Unitarians; and he stood firm: "I have something besides abstract speculations and dry moral precepts, or mysterious jargon to offer. I have the doctrine of Life, the Word of Life to proclaim. I have an end to gain; it is to bring men into communion with each other, so that the Word of Life may have free course among them, and be glorified in binding them together in that love wherewith God hath loved us."[56]

Although his views no longer conformed with those of his fellow Unitarians, Brownson made no attempt at this time to leave their fold. He helped establish the Transcendentalist experiment at Brook Farm, a cooperative settlement at West Roxbury, Massachusetts. He wrote in praise of it and even sent his son Henry to live there.[57] But how could Brownson be at home with Transcendentalists? He saw man capable of sin; they regarded man as sinless. He viewed religion as objective; they looked upon religion as an inward, subjective emotion.[58] Being neither popular nor happy at Brook Farm, Brownson's stay was short-lived.[59]

In 1843 Brownson wrote a series of articles on "The Mission of Jesus" for the new weekly journal, *The Christian World*. These articles are significant in his thinking because in each article he arrives closer to the acceptance of Roman Catholicism, the religious faith he was to espouse until his death. Brownson had not foreseen finding himself at the very doorsteps of Roman Catholicism when he began these articles. He even hesitated to acquiesce in the conclusions to which his arguments had led him.

In this series of essays he sought to develop and apply to the explanation of Christianity his doctrine of life or communion. The mediatorial life of Christ, he emphasized, is the life between God and man. Acceptance of Christ joins man to God and makes possible man's redemption. Christ as the God-Man is the medium of communion between God and man. But, as Brownson pursued and expatiated this basic thought, he arrived at the need of a Church as the living Body of Christ today, which dispenses to mankind and makes possible for mankind participation in the mediatorial life of Christ.

The first four articles on "The Mission of Jesus" pleased his Protestant friends. *The New Churchman*, edited by Dr. Samuel Seabury, felt that Brownson's views were leading Puritan Boston into a new era.[60] Subsequent articles received favorable remarks on the part of Roman Catholics, who published selected portions of them in their own periodicals.

The eighth essay in the series sought to answer the question, "Which is the true church or body of Christ?" Brownson's logic led him to the belief that all communion of the different Christian sects with one another, including the Roman Catholic Church, had not been completely interrupted: "They all belong, in some sort, to the one and the same family, and all, in a measure, live the life of Christ."[61] For obvious reasons, *The Christian World* refused to publish this last article, and Brownson declined offers of a Roman Catholic editor to publish it. He was not yet convinced in his searching mind that Roman Catholicism was the true living Body of Christ on earth.

Realizing his tendencies to Roman Catholicism, yet still not desirous of uniting himself to the Roman Church, he sought for some compromise or middle ground. Here was his dilemma:

> I regarded the apostolic see as the central source of the Christian life; but the body seemed to me to have been broken into fragments, and to exist no longer in its integrity. The Catholic Church was undoubtedly the larger fragment, the one through which the main current of the divine-human life continued to flow; but no man would dare say that nothing of that life is or can be lived outside of her communion, and I had found no Catholic that held there could be absolutely no salvation outside of it.[62]

Even though the articles logically concluded that the Catholic Church is the true Church or the living body of Christ, Brownson hesitated at least a year before accepting that faith and instruction in it. He had rejected the claims of Roman Catholicism because he could not follow what appeared to be the logic of his own thinking.

A number of reasons presented obstacles which had to be overcome in his restless mind. The Reformation could not be without cause and the Protestant movement completely wrong. He entertained a poor opinion of the Roman Catholic writers who were always engrossed in "mere technicalities and verbal distinctions."[63] He still saw much truth in the popular Protestant belief that the Catholic countries of Europe were unprogressive compared to the non-Catholic countries. In the Catholic clergy, trained in what he termed a "supernatural scholasticism," he found lacking the leadership to extend social progress and freedom and a tendency to abdicate itself to the side of absolutism, known for keeping the masses in slavery and ignorance. Furthermore, up to this time he had read only two Catholic books, Milner's *End of Controversy* and the *Catechism of the Council of Trent*.

One may wonder why Brownson, known for passing from one religion to another, could not now pass into Roman Catholicism. He regarded his previous changes of Protestant religious denominations as "little more than going from one apartment to another in the same house."[64] A transition to Catholicism constituted a major break, an entrance into "a new and untried region."[65] He could not as yet fully comprehend the doctrine of the infallibility of the Pope, although he granted infallibility to the Church as the source of divine life. A major break was seen as necessary for Brownson. Christian life flowed into the life of any Christian. Undoubtedly he regarded the Roman Catholic Church as the main current through which flows the divine-human life of Christ; for it was the first and the largest of the Christian sects. The other sects, however, even upon breaking off from the main current, retained a certain amount of Christian life. Thus Brownson toyed with the idea of seeking to effect the union of all Christian sects and possibly to restore the body of Christ to its original unfragmented unity. He had to delay his acceptance of Roman Catholicism until his mind could search no further.

Yet Brownson pondered the future of his soul. "Suppose I die before I have effected the reunion of Christendom—what will become of my own soul? I am engaged in a good work, but what if I became a castaway?"[66] He had concluded by logic that the Roman Catholic Church was clearly the Church of history, the true body of Christ today. Rather than keep his mind in unsettled doubt he arranged in May, 1844, with Bishop Benedict J. Fenwick of Boston for a discussion of his possible entrance into the Catholic Church. Bishop Fenwick recommended him to his coadjutor and subsequent successor, Bishop John B. Fitzpatrick, who became Brownson's instructor. Bishop Fitzpatrick had to overcome a degree of distrust and prejudice towards Brownson. He regarded the prospective convert as proud and conceited and even doubted Brownson's motives for seeking admission into the Catholic Church. After several months of instruction, however, Fitzpatrick became convinced of Brownson's sincerity.

Although it was the doctrine of life and communion that led Brownson to the door of the Catholic Church, it was belief in the Church's divine commission to teach all men and nations in matters affecting eternal salvation that actually became the rational basis for his complete acceptance. The doctrine of sharing the divine-human life of Christ could pertain to any person claiming to be a Christian. But the doctrine of divine commission through apostolic succession pin-pointed a definite authority to whom to submit. So Brownson delineated the final convincing argument that led to his conversion to Catholicism: "To believe what the church teaches, because she teaches it, is in this, the Catholic view of the question, perfectly reasonable, because her teaching really is authority for reason, testimony to the understanding, as well as a command to the will. Authority for believing is always necessary, and nothing is more unreasonable than to believe without authority."[67]

V *Roman Catholicism*

On October 20, 1844, Brownson was formally received into the Catholic Church by Bishop Fitzpatrick, as were his wife and children subsequently. Despite occasional misunderstandings with fellow Catholics, he testified in his biography that he never regretted the step; he had found a religious faith that he could adhere to without doubt until death.[68]

Brownson had discontinued preaching early in 1844 before applying for instructions in the Catholic faith. Income from lectures and the *Quarterly Review* became the only means to provide for his large family. Upon conversion, he considered discontinuing publication of the *Quarterly Review* and entering some other field, possibly law. Bishop Fitzpatrick, however, urged him to retain the publication. Despite Brownson's own admission of little knowledge of Catholic theology, the bishop succeeded in convincing Brownson of the opportunity to work for the conversion of his fellow Americans. He saw in Brownson a bold champion for Catholicity, one most able to point out the compatibility of Catholic doctrine with American democratic principles of government. Such a role also offered Brownson a means of reparation and atonement for advocating errors in the past. Study in Catholic theology under Bishop Fitzpatrick's tutelage followed for some months. St. Thomas Aquinas' and St. Augustine's works supplemented Brownson's rudimentary knowledge acquired in instructions before his admission to Catholicism.

The immediate task of the *Quarterly Review* after his conversion to Roman Catholicism became the defense of his new faith, especially by the critical analyses of current Protestant theological writings. Some members of the Catholic faith questioned the somewhat authoritative tone of a recent convert and layman writing on theological matters. But Brownson assured his readers that "he does not speak from his own head, but under the revision of those who are neither laymen nor converts."[69] Bishop Fitzpatrick, who had urged his continuance of the *Review*, supervised the articles on theology.

About 1849 Brownson decided to make the *Review* less theological; for it obviously could not be the conversion of Protestants that he hoped for in his theological writings. Most of the Protestant readers had withdrawn their subscriptions upon his conversion to Catholicism. He believed now that the great social questions of the day ought to be discussed from a Catholic viewpoint. Besides, supervision was not required for non-theological articles, and he could proceed to "writing from himself rather than according to order."[70] These non-theological articles are discussed in subsequent chapters devoted to his socio-economic and political thought.

With hardly any Protestant readers Brownson appealed to Roman Catholics for "a firm and bold profession of their faith, and an independent and fearless, though quiet, assertion of their rights as Christians, as citizens, as men."[71] One cannot help admiring in his early writings as a Roman Catholic the competence he displayed in Catholic theology and his power of analyzing what he now considered errors to which he had previously adhered.

The intrepid defense and advocacy of Catholicism in his articles brought him a well-cherished approbation from the American Catholic hierarchy. The bishops attending the Provincial Council of Baltimore in May, 1849, addressed to him a special letter of encouragement and approval, which Brownson proudly published in his *Quarterly*. At Bishop Fitzpatrick's recommendation Pope Pius IX also sent Brownson a letter of approbation in April, 1854, which he also placed in his *Review* in both English and Latin. Without this ecclesiastical approval Brownson had to admit that the future of his *Quarterly* was in serious jeopardy, for circulation had been drastically reduced since the end of 1845.

As Brownson's stand on the social questions of the day— particularly on nativism, the parochial schools, and the rights of the temporal and spiritual authorities—brought him into open conflict with many of his co-religionists, his popularity and influence began to wane considerably. Bishop Fitzpatrick's failure to stand by him on a number of issues led Brownson to consider leaving Boston. He chose to move to New York in October, 1855, from where he also continued to publish his *Quarterly*. He anticipated a freer opportunity and better cooperation in this new environment.[72] Catholics of New York acknowledged their pleasure in having him in their midst; they attended his lectures in great numbers. Subsequent invitations to lecture on the role of Catholicism in America were received from Catholic groups in St. Louis, Charleston, Chicago, Savannah.

Brownson's hope for encouragement from episcopal authority, however, was short-lived. His too liberal views for American Catholic churchmen led Archbishop John Hughes of New York to voice disapproval at a commencement address at Fordham University (then known as St. John's College) in 1856. As Archbishop Hughes had succeeded Brownson at the rostrum, Brownson regarded the occasion for the disapproval as most embarrassing and devastating to his personal pride. Writing to Archbishop Hughes he commented: "There was no equality in the case. It was crushing me with the weight of authority in a matter of simple opinion."[73] And in referring to Hughes several years later, he noted how the archbishop had firmly stated to him, "I will suffer no man in my diocese that I cannot control. I will either put him down or he shall put me down."[74]

Even though Archbishop Hughes disclaimed any personal animosity toward Brownson, he went on to rebuke the *Review* for its too militant expression of the author's ideas to Americanize the Catholic Church. Once again Brownson felt that he needed a new setting for his work. He therefore moved to Elizabeth, New Jersey, in 1857, under the jurisdiction of Bishop James Roosevelt Bayley of Newark (later Archbishop of Baltimore). In Bishop Bayley, himself a convert, he hoped for a better understanding of his views. Pleased with the release from Bishop Fitzpatrick's censorship and from Archbishop Hughes's desire to restrain his views, Brownson later wrote: "We attained to that intellectual freedom which we had first asserted the church allows, demands and secures. We thus recovered the broken link of our life, reunited our present life with our life prior to our conversion, and resumed, so to speak, our personal identity."[75]

Adding to a mistrust of his socio-economic and political views (to be considered in detail in subsequent chapters) was Brownson's theory of knowledge. The commonly accepted view of how man arrives at a knowledge of God to which Roman Catholics adhered was based on St. Thomas Aquinas: the existence of God is not immediately self-evident or an innate truth, but one attainable by means of the human mind reasoning from the effects it observes to the Cause responsible for these effects. Brownson would argue that man has an intuitive knowledge of God; for in the very act of thought itself man perceives that there exists a reality apart from himself, which has been created and needs, therefore, a creator.[76] Brownson was classified as an ontologist for such a view. Ontologism was regarded as a position theologically untenable for Roman Catholics; for, in having God known by intuition, God would be confused with His creatures. Such a conclusion, the opponents of ontologism held, results into the error of pantheism. Furthermore, Brownson had employed phrases of the leading ontologist of the day, Vincenzo Gioberti, who had been censured by Rome for his views. Brownson denied being an ontologist but claimed that the true position of man's knowledge of God lay between ontologism and scholasticism. Brownson would deem it impossible for human reason to conclude that God exists without first in some way having a suspicion of His existence. His view of intuition was not the same as cognition, as the ontologists confused the terms. Moreover, man's first suspicion of God had later to be examined by logic, if he were at all to believe in a Supreme Being.[77]

Brownson, however, was never able to remove the stigma of ontologism from his beliefs. In the minds of many, despite his denials, he had praised Gioberti's philosophy too often and too strongly to declare himself completely uninfluenced by an erroneous approach to man's knowledge of God.[78]

Losing his faith in the unbounded liberty advocated by the liberalism of the nineteenth century, a form of liberty which he regarded as an example of satanic intervention led Brownson in 1854 to write *The Spirit-Rapper: An Autobiography*. He personifies in the characters of this novel many of the acquaintances of his life, among whom are Fanny Wright, Emerson, Alcott, Theodore Parker. By modern literary classification the work is a novel but Brownson himself was somewhat puzzled as to how to classify it: "It is not a novel; it is not a romance; it is not a biography of a real individual; it is not a dissertation, an essay, or a regular treatise; and yet it perhaps has some elements of them all, thrown together in just such a way as best suited my convenience, or my purpose."[79]

Theodore Maynard considers this book of Brownson as "without doubt the worst," both because its story is deficient and because it gives the impression of being hurriedly written.[80] But the real purpose of the work becomes meaningful only after analyses of what Brownson regarded as failures in his life and of the difficulties he encountered despite his sincerity of purpose.

After his conversion to Roman Catholicism, Brownson decided that the great social questions of the day ought to be discussed from a Catholic point of view, a matter in which he felt the Catholic press to be deficient. The retaliatory remarks of Catholic journalists only led to a lessening of his influence, resulting in a brief suspension of his *Quarterly Review*. A priest further published a work entitled *The Atheism of Brownson's Review*, accusing him of heretical tendencies and of too much dependence on philosophers not thoroughly Catholic. Brownson's appeal to Bishop Fitzpatrick of Boston for a clarification of his theological soundness went unheeded; he was told merely to expect criticism.

The articles in the *Review* setting forth the doctrine that obedience to the state was justified only when it meant obedience to God brought censure, as well as the accusation that he was an ultramontanist, from Bishop O'Connor of Pittsburgh and from Bishop Purcell of Cincinnati.

Brownson found himself in further disrepute among most of his fellow Roman Catholics because of his tackling of the Nativist movement and the Know-Nothing party. Infuriated at the unreasonableness of the charges that Catholics could not be good Americans, he wrote: "The sentiment which underlies native Americanism is as strong in the bosom of American Catholics as it is in the bosom of American Protestants."[81] Yet he appealed to his fellow Catholics to make the Church more American and less Irish, believing that the progress and influence of the Church in this country depended on its ability to acclimate itself to a new culture. For such an appeal he was denounced for enkindling anti-Irish sentiment.[82] In discouragement Brownson wrote to a friend: "I own I have lost some of my first fervor with regard to a portion of the American Catholic body. They have so misrepresented me, and are so ready to seize every opportunity to blacken my character, that I do not feel that lively confidence in them that I did."[83]

Written with this background the *Spirit-Rapper* becomes for Brownson his theology of history. For despite one's good efforts and the power of God in history, there exists evil constantly thwarting good; the devil and his forces also are at work.

The hero of the book, the Spirit-Rapper, undoubtedly Brownson himself, is introduced by one of his friends to mesmerism, a method of sending a person into a trance by the use of suggestions and movements of the hand.[84] Although the hero at first laughed at its possibility, he became convinced when mesmeric experiments were performed in his presence and he concluded that man possesses a mysterious power which science has yet to explore fully, the demonic power of human nature.[85] The hero, furthermore, found that with instruction he was able to mesmerize himself and others. Employing an experiment in which he was the subject, he ended up by believing in and even advancing ideas diametrically opposed to views he had previously held. But, since the Spirit-Rapper preferred to use this power for good and since God will work with and for us only if we work with and for Him, he determined to use this power for promoting good by becoming a philanthropist and world-reformer. He announced his program: "Break the fetters which now bind the people, emancipate them from their masters, assert their supremacy, and establish their power, which of course in the last analysis will be our power over them. They will then reorganize society, religion, and politics, and every thing else, after the best model, and in the way which will best meet our wishes."[86]

Although his program of philanthropic reform was in the best tradition of human progress, the Spirit-Rapper had to admit that not all who sought to influence others were sincere and noble in their purpose. For mesmerism was of two kinds: natural and Satanic; and it was not always an easy task to distinguish between them. Satan, or the devil, might possess this power. Brownson rejects the charge that there is any tendency to superstition in mesmerism. It would be superstitious to attribute supernatural intervention to what can be explained on natural principles.

Santanic intervention is invidious. It presents evil in the guise of good. It appeals to the weaknesses of human nature, most notably a "sickly philanthropy."[87] Brownson points out in the novel the teachings of Christianity, the references in Sacred Scripture to the existence and the power of the devil. He recalls the rite of the Sacrament of Baptism in which "the unclean spirit" is ordered to leave the baptized, and the appointment of exorcists, whose duty it is to drive out evil spirits from human beings.

Although expecting derision for his notion of spirit-rapping, Brownson found an explanation for his failures and misunderstandings. Mingled with the imaginative tales that he related is a strong conviction that Satan had sought to thwart his sincere efforts. Thus this novel cannot be so readily dismissed as mere "fun and fancy free." It does offer a moral and rationalization when analyzed against the background of the events in Brownson's life.[88]

The Convert; or Leaves from My Experience is Brownson's autobiography. Written in 1857, it was dedicated to Bishop John B. Fitzpatrick of Boston, his instructor in the Catholic faith. In it Brownson traces his religious convictions and experiences to his admission into the Roman Catholic Church. With all the candor and intellectual honesty at his disposal, he offers for the reader, both Catholic and non-Catholic, the various stages in the development of his religious thought.

Brownson felt he had to write such a work. Non-Catholics questioned his logic; Catholics, his sincerity. In 1854 he had written *The Spirit-Rapper* in which he had portrayed his reaction to misunderstandings of his motives. But this work could hardly compare with the seriousness of tone and with the depth of the logical and psychological explanations of his thoughts and attitudes as presented in *The Convert*.

For non-Catholics Brownson saw a need for a thorough analysis of his theological development. Characteristic of his friends' feelings toward his conversion to Roman Catholicism was that of James Freeman Clarke, who had written that it was "hardly worthwhile to exert our ingenuity in exposing the fallacy of arguments, which, judging by experience, Mr. Brownson would himself be ready to confute in the course of a year or two. No man has ever equalled Mr. Brownson in the ability with which he has refuted his own arguments."[89]

In a sermon Theodore Parker pictured Brownson as a

man of unbalanced mind, intellectual always, but spiritual never; heady, but not hearty; roving from Church to Church; now Trinitarian, then unbeliever, then Universalist, Unitarian, Catholic—everything by turns but nothing long; seeking rest by turning perpetually over and becoming at last a man having experienced many theologies but never a religion; not a Christian, but only a verbal index of Christianity—a commonplace book of theology.[90]

Evaluations of this type necessitated a justification for his conversion to Roman Catholicism. Brownson found further assurance in the fact that he was writing from nearly thirteen years of stability in this religious denomination.[91]

But Brownson's arguments were not convincing. The *Biblical Repertory and Princeton Review* in January, 1858, offered a disparaging critique of *The Convert*. It argued as follow:

It requires no slight courage in one man to set himself up as the expounder and champion of the multitudinous and contradictory systems which our author has successively espoused and repudiated. But it requires still greater courage to attempt, as he has done in this volume, to vindicate his moral integrity and intellectual consistency in such a course. It is somewhat of an exploit to appear as the advocate of nearly every type of opinion, except evangelical truth—to career through the whole compass of fatuous error, from the credulity of Atheism to the credulity of Superstition. But it is a still more prodigious exploit for such a man to undertake to expound and justify himself.[92]

As far as non-Catholics were concerned, Brownson had changed his religious views too often to assure stability of thought. Granted even a closed mind on the part of the above quoted Presbyterian journal, non-Catholic evaluation of *The Convert* was characteristically expressed in an editorial in the New York *Herald*: "What Weathercock Brownson says or does is of very little consequence to the community at large. Brownson has blown from all points of the compass in religion and in politics."[93] And he had also offended too often many Catholics, especially those of the hierarchy, for his *apologia* to acquire for him any immediate desired vindication.

Even after publication of *The Convert* and a renewed interest in social questions, Brownson continued his masterly articles in defense of Catholicism and his discussions of theological topics. Among the many issues with which he dealt were evolution and the Reformation.

The publication of Charles Darwin's *Origin of the Species* in 1859 signaled for many the classifying of religion as pious superstition. Evolution was believed to contradict the Bible account of the creation of the world and of man. In answering the charges of the adherents of evolution, some theologians went to the extreme position of repudiating science when it conflicted with religious belief. But Brownson maintained from the very start of the controversy a balanced *via media*. He disagreed with the theologians whose arguments he felt appealed only to those "who care nothing for science or civilization, for human intelligence and social well-being, and whose faith having been entertained without reason, no reason can disturb."[94] Yet he placed limitations on the conclusions that science can deduce from its experiments and theories. The realm of absolute truth, as contained in the Scriptures, science cannot contradict. Faith deals with spiritual reality; science only with what is evident to the senses. "In all that is contingent," Brownson reasoned, "reason has need of experience, observation, experiment, investigation; but with these alone, we can never rise above the empirical, or attain to scientific results."[95]

Writing several years later, Brownson even more clearly delineates the limitations of science: "We do not deduce our physics from metaphysics, but our metaphysics or philosophy gives the law to the inductive or empirical sciences and prescribes the bounds beyond which they cannot pass without ceasing to be sciences."[96] He, therefore, condemned atheistic evolution as it failed to distinguish between man, a rational creature with a soul and a consequent moral responsibility, and beast, an irrational animal not considered a morally responsible being.[97] Brownson's critique of the rash scientists of his day can well be appreciated:

> The greater part of what our advanced thinkers call science, consists not only of assumptions, but of assumptions hardly made before they are modified or rejected for others equally baseless, to be in their turn modified or rejected. . . . Indeed, our scientists regard science, as our freelovers regard marriage, as simply provisory, and would be disgusted with it if not at liberty to be constantly changing it. They regard truth as variable as their own moods and views.[98]

Brownson's "Essays on the Reformation" also takes a stand between extreme views: those of Protestantism and those of Roman Catholicism.[99] His son Henry considered the three essays on this topic among the best of his father's writings.[100] In these essays—occasioned by the refutation of the volumes of the Swiss Calvinist J. Merle d'Aubigné on the Reformation by Bishop John L. Spalding, then of Louisville, Kentucky—Brownson pointed out the erroneous *a priori* judgments of each writer. D'Aubigné regarded the Roman Catholic Church as satanic and Protestantism as divine; Spalding regarded Protestantism as satanic and the Roman Catholic Church as divine.

Although writing from the point of view of a Catholic, Brownson nevertheless calls for a more objective historical approach to a study and evaluation of the Reformation. His starting point would be to view the Protestant movement as originating within the Church and not outside of it; for the reformers were at first members of the Church. Nor would Brownson paint the Catholic Church as immaculate in the sixteenth century; reform was acknowledged by many as necessary for both leaders and members of the Church. "But Protestantism was an unforeseen, unexpected, and unintended accident. It was neither foreseen nor designed.[101] If Luther had not received the support of secular princes, the momentum necessary for the sharp break that took place would not have been lasting. Brownson felt that the real reformation was Catholic and not Protestant: "Its normal development was eminently Catholic, and found expression in the doctrinal definitions and reformatory decrees of the Council of Trent."[102]

His uncompromising and bold views as a journalist did not help the circulation of his *Quarterly*. His articles on Catholic parochial schools did not please the Catholic hierarchy. The manner in which he dealt with the slavery question embittered many of his fellow Catholics toward him, especially Archbishop Hughes of New York. Disagreement with Hughes on the relationship between the temporal and the spiritual powers even led to denunciation on the part of the American hierarchy at Rome and a discrediting among Catholics that resulted in suspension of the *Quarterly* in 1864.[103]

After the suspension of the *Quarterly*, Brownson was left without a publication of his own to express his views. But a number of influential Catholics still saw in him a staunch advocate of the faith and a writer of extraordinary talent. The Very Reverend Edward Sorin, founder of the University of Notre Dame, established the *Ave Maria* magazine in 1865 to extend devotion to the Blessed Virgin Mary as Mother of Christ. Brownson was subsequently invited to write a series of articles on the Blessed Virgin, which confined themselves not merely to devotional practice in her honor but also to setting forth a philosophical explanation of the principles underlying such devotion. Articles also were written weekly for almost six months on the veneration of the saints, images, and relics. In 1866 Brownson wrote a series on the moral and social influence of devotion to the Mother of Christ.

The *Catholic World*, which also began publication in 1865, requested the services of Brownson. Its editor-in-chief, Isaac Hecker, a convert to Catholicism, had been a friend of Brownson for many years. Translating articles from foreign languages at first constituted most of Brownson's work for this magazine, but he later wrote articles more conciliatory in tone than those which had been written before the suspension of the *Quarterly*. He also published articles in the New York *Tablet;* in these he modified earlier views on the ineffectiveness of Catholic education to train for American Catholic leadership and the supremacy of the spiritual over the temporal, a position which influenced non-Catholics to mistrust American Catholics. These modified views found ready acceptance by the Catholic hierarchy, clergy, and laity.[104]

Independent of mind as he was, Brownson naturally preferred being his own editor instead of a contributor. He subsequently revived the *Quarterly Review* in 1873. Sobered by so many past controversies and desirous of providing a tone more acceptable to readers, Brownson began the first issue of the revived *Reiew* by claiming:

> I willingly admit that I made many mistakes; but I regard as the greatest of all the mistakes into which I fell during the last three or four years that I published my *Review,* that of holding back the stronger points of the Catholic faith, on which I had previously insisted; of laboring to present Catholicity in a form as little repulsive to my non-Catholic countrymen as possible; and of insisting on only the minimum of Catholicity, or what had been expressly defined by the Holy See or a general council. I am not likely to fall into that mistake again.[105]

Brownson went on further to disclaim any attachment to the tenets or spirit of liberalism, which he now branded as a polite name for sedition, rebellion, and revolutionism.

Brownson continued his *Review* in a less belligerent tone for three years until November, 1875. Poor health forced him to relinquish its publication, since he found reading difficult because of failing eyesight and writing an impossibility because of stiffening of the joints in his hands. Some of his last articles had to be dictated. Unable to continue his work, Brownson left Elizabeth, New Jersey, and retired to live with his son Henry in Detroit, Michigan. His health became increasingly worse, and he died a few months later on Easter Monday, April 17,

1876, having received the Last Sacraments of the Roman Catholic Church on the previous day.

Although his funeral services were conducted at St. Anne's Church and he was interred in the Catholic cemetery of Mount Elliot, both in Detroit, the University of Notre Dame requested ten years later that his remains be brought to a specially constructed Brownson Memorial Chapel in Sacred Heart Church on the campus of the university. The epitaph marking his resting place forcibly describes the ideals for which he lived and wrote, a belated but genuine esteem that his fellow Roman Catholics could express.

HIC JACET

ORESTES

A

BROWNSON

QUI VERAM FIDEM HUMILITER AGNOVIT

INTEGRAM VIXIT VITAM

CALAMO LINGUAQUE

ECCLESIAM AC PATRIAM

FORTITER DEFENDIT

AC LICET MORTI CORPUS ABIERIT

MENTIS OPERA SUPERSUNT

IMMORTALIA

INGENII MONUMENTA[106]

CHAPTER *2*

The Social Reformer

AS A UNIVERSALIST PREACHER Brownson saw in the
Christian Gospel more than just a message to be preached on
Sundays. He envisioned Christianity as also a social movement,
influencing man's day by day struggle to earn a livelihood. The
reading of William Godwin's *The Inquiry concerning Political
Justice and its Influence on General Virtue and Happiness,* published in 1793, had alerted Brownson's mind to the social injustices of the day and the inability of society as organized to
cope with the attendant social problems. But the excessive
individualism of Godwin in his concept of all government as a
usurpation of the individual's authority led Brownson to believe
that under the conditions put forth by Godwin a state of anarchy,
worse than the savage state, would befall mankind. He sympathized with Godwin's analysis of social inequities but re-
frained from his suggested means to cure them.[1]

I *The Social Radical*

In October, 1829, Brownson attended a lecture by Frances
Wright on the evils of society, in Utica, New York. This young
Scotswoman had come to the United States in 1818 and had
offered Americans a plan to emancipate the slaves, which gained
the interest of Jefferson and Madison. She regarded slavery,
however, as indicative of a far more basic failure of Americans—
their inability to apprehend the far-reaching role of environment
in the shaping of man's place in society. These ideas and Fannie's
eloquent charm led Brownson to converse with her after the
lecture, which began their friendship.

Wright and Brownson found that they both leaned toward the
writings of English utopian, Robert Owen. Moreover, Wright

was publishing the *Free Enquirer* in New York with Owen's son, Robert Dale Owen. Sharing the same inclinations, Brownson readily accepted the offer to become a corresponding editor of the *Free Enquirer*. The Owen major premise consisted in the belief that man was but a passive creature of the circumstances in which he found himself. A program of reform would seek to lift him above his unfortunate status. This would be done by a plan of "state guardianship," in which the state would embark upon a program of education for all children, beginning with the age of two; they would be kept in boarding schools, until the age of sixteen. Furthermore, no distinction was to be made between children of the rich and of the poor in these state-supported schools.

The Workingmen's Party in New York was regarded as a logical means for achieving the Owenite goals. But Brownson and Wright failed in their efforts to influence the workingmen to associate themselves with Owen's ideas. Meanwhile, Brownson's active interest in these radical measures led to his leaving the Universalist fold and to his resigning from the editorship of the *Gospel Advocate*.

The year 1830 was a significant one for Brownson. It was marked by his loss of faith in God and in the Workingmen's Party. His bout with religious skepticism has been told. He also became disheartened with the Owen-Wright program, for he considered the state-supported system of education as an infringement of the rights and the role of the family in the bringing up of children. He, therefore, severed his connection with the *Free Enquirer* and with the extreme radical views of Owen and Wright.

But Brownson never lost hope for effecting social reform. Returning to the pulpit, this time as a Unitarian, he saw in moral reform the basis for social reform. In an address on July 4, 1831, he declared, " 'Tis the slavery of the mind which paves the way to that of the body, and the slavery of individuals which induces that of nations."[2] In an article for the *Unitarian* in 1834 he wrote in a thoroughly social Christian manner:

To effect any real reform, the individual man must be improved. . . . The reformer's concern is with the individual. That which gives the individual a free mind, a pure heart, and full scope for just and beneficent action, is that which will reform the many. When the majority of any community are fitted for better institutions, for a more advanced state of society, that state will be introduced, and those institutions will be secured.[3]

Brownson's views on and interest in social reform attracted the attention of his fellow Unitarian preachers, William Ellery Channing and George Ripley. At their suggestion he came to Boston as an independent preacher to evangelize the laboring class. In May and June of 1836 he conducted religious meetings in Boston's Lyceum Hall. In a sermon entitled "The Wants of the Times," Brownson called Christ "the prophet of the workingman" and asked for social reform based on the teachings of Christianity.[4] He impressed many with his eloquence and forthright stand, and an English observer wrote of him: "The people are requiring a better clergy. Even in Boston, as far behind the country as that city is, a notable change has already taken place. A strong man, full of enlarged sympathies, has not only discerned the wants of the time, but set himself to do what one man may to supply them."[5]

With a following assured, Brownson established the Society for Christian Union and Progress for Boston's workingmen. As a guide for this organization he published *New Views of Christianity, Society and the Church*.[6] His independence found an opportunity to advance itself as he called for a new Church, a synthesis of all others yet independent of them—the Church of the Future, which he undoubtedly would head.

But the Church of the Future never became a reality. Yet it was observed that "the rising up of this new church in Boston is an eloquent sign of the times."[7] Three hundred to five hundred listened to his discourses every Sunday from 1836 to his conversion to Roman Catholicism in 1844. *New Views*, however, created no theological stir. Men listened with the hope of social reform, not for the institution of a new Church. As a matter of fact, Brownson even gave evidence of abandoning his approach to social reform by individual moral reform; for he saw that social conditions can influence moral behavior: "In some states of society there must be a social growth before there can be—in relation to a part of the community—an individual growth."[8] It was useless to preach the power of prayer when the power to earn a living did not exist.

Economic conditions brought on by the Panic of 1837, moreover, convinced Brownson that action was necessary. In that
year banks suspended operation and failed, factories closed, and
a depression put many laborers out of work. Class war, he
sensed, was on the rise; and he noted that "all classes, each in
turn, have possessed the government; and the time has come for
all predominance of class to end; for Man, the People to rule."⁹
Identifying the Whigs as the party of the greedy money-class,
he made no secret of his political affiliation and declared himself a Democrat. For "in the last analysis the dominant idea of
the Whigs is not *Man,* but *Property;* and the contest between
them and the democracy was rightly declared . . . to be a contest between *Man* and *Money*."¹⁰ He therefore asked the
churches to back the people's cause against the money-class since
he believed that the Democratic Party was closer to the ideals
of Christ's Gospel.¹¹ The Whigs, he argued, developed their
tenets from the atheistic tendencies of Hobbes.¹² With political
parties necessary, since man could not labor for his goals as an
individual, man must strive for social and economic progress in
the party sharing those same goals which, for Brownson, were
obtainable only through the Democratic Party.¹³

For the presidential election of 1840 the Whigs nominated at
their convention William Henry Harrison for President and John
Tyler for vice-president. Martin Van Buren became the standard-
bearer for the Democrats. Brownson aligned himself with the
Democrats in the campaign: "I have a fellow feeling . . . with
all who struggle against power and seek to secure for the people
a portion of their long lost liberty."¹⁴ To aid the Democrats in
the ensuing presidential race, he published one of his most
controversial essays, "The Laboring Classes."

In strong, unequivocal language Brownson's essay chastises the
lot that industrial capitalism has imposed on the workingman.
Not even the injustices of slavery in the South compare to those
of the laborer in the North. Under the pretext of paying wages
the industrial capitalist assuages his conscience for the deplorable working conditions of his "slaves." The slave in the South,
admittedly a possession of his master, at least enjoys a guarantee
from the uncertainties of employment. "Wages," in Brownson's
way of thinking, "is a cunning device of the devil, for the benefit
of tender consciences, who would retain all the advantages of the

slave system, without the expense, trouble, and odium of being slave-holders."[15] He portrays the industrial capitalist of America in the nineteenth century in the following words:

> The man who employs them, and for whom they are toiling as so many slaves is one of our city nabobs, revelling in luxury; or he is a member of our legislature, enacting laws to put money in his own pocket; or he is a member of Congress, contending for a high Tariff to tax the poor for the benefit of the rich; or in these times he is shedding crocodile tears over the deplorable condition of the poor laborer, while he docks his wages twenty-five per cent; building miniature log cabins, shouting Harrison and "hard cider." And this man would fain pass for a Christian and a republican. He shouts for liberty, stickles for equality, and is horrified at a Southern planter who keeps slaves.[16]

As emancipation must be fought for the Southern slave, so it also must be fought for the workingman. This would require the opportunity for a laborer to amass sufficient capital so as to venture his own business and free him from continued subservience to a capitalist overlord. Appropriate government action must be taken to accomplish this goal: the rooting out of monopolies, the discontinuing of the system of credit on the part of banks, the abolishing of the inheritance of property, and the repealing of all laws that burden the laboring class. Brownson obviously did not expect the rich to approve his plan of emancipation for the workingman but expressed hope for its adoption only by the use of physical force: "It will be effected only by the strong arm of physical force. It will come, if it ever come at all, only at the conclusion of war, the like of which the world as yet has never witnessed, and from which, however, inevitable it may seem to the eye of philosophy, the heart of Humanity recoils with horror."[17]

Commenting on "The Laboring Classes," Schlesinger regards it as "perhaps the best study of the workings of society by an American before the Civil War." For its analysis of and insight into the social and economic problems of industrial capitalism Schlesinger adds that "no other American of the day and few Europeans inquired so deeply into the weaknesses and contradictions of industrial society."[18] Brownson's essay may have served as a means of alerting labor to the injustices of its place in society. It may be considered an expedient piece of propaganda so characteristic of political campaigning, but Brownson did show a lack of understanding of the impact that the Industrial Revolution had already begun to have in manufacturing and commerce. Successful and intensive industrialization required large quantities of capital to build factories and machines, to buy raw materials, and to utilize available manpower. With all its attendant evils, industrial capitalism needed a certain amount of bigness to become effective. Brownson, in condemning the evils, sought destruction of the system. More to the truth in evaluating Brownson's essay would be to describe him in the words of Schlesinger as Marx's "nearest forerunner in America."[19] For, as Professor H. S. Foxwell, in the introduction to Anton Menger's *The Right to the Whole Produce of Labour,* has written, "This is socialism of the true Marxian type."[20]

Brownson's essay on the laboring classes, regarded as too revolutionary, became a campaign issue in the election of 1840. The Whigs quickly classified it as evidence of the socialist tendencies of the Democrats. The Democrats, in turn, staunchly disavowed its ideas and dismissed Brownson as in any way a spokesman of their party. Religious leaders and the periodicals of the day attacked Brownson's charges as exaggerations and his views as social radicalism, even calling him a Jacobin and an American Robespierre.[21]

No amount of criticism, however, could ever shake Brownson's convictions. In October, 1840, he proceeded with a second article on "The Laboring Classes." Property again became the focal point of attack. In an agricultural society, he stated, men could be both capitalists and laborers; no division and, therefore, no discord would exist between the two classes. Industrial capitalism has made class divisions inevitable, and government always favors property in its legislation. He reiterated his proposal to abolish the inheritance of property as a sure means to insure equality: "We believe property should be held subordinate to man, and not man to property; and therefore that it is always lawful to make such modifications of its constitution as the good of Humanity requires."[22]

But after the blistering attacks of the first essay and its rejection by the Democrats whom the essay was meant to help, the second essay on "The Laboring Classes" died the death of those writings which lack readers.

Election day came in November, 1840, with 234 electoral votes for Harrison and sixty for Van Buren. These results embittered Brownson, who had placed so much hope in the people. He lost faith in the people, who failed to demonstrate faith in their own party. How could he champion the cause of the people if the people themselves would not rally behind their own party?

Despite the election of 1840, Brownson continued asking for the defeat of Whig efforts to bolster business interests by setting up the national bank, increasing tariffs, and strengthening the powers of the Federal Government. What success could the opposition have against the Whigs? He wrote in despondency: "As yet, history so far as we are acquainted, presents no instance of a political contest, in which man has remained the victor over property."[23] Because of his loss of faith in the people as their own rulers, he began a reappraisal of the American democratic system of government and a formulation of his own political thought. But for the time being he saw no place for himself in practical politics. Man could not decide what was good for himself; he belonged basically by inheritance from Adam to a race of sinners. It must take time for sinful creatures to see and choose the good.[24] Brownson gave himself to the writing of *The Mediatorial Life of Jesus,* wherein he reverts to the role of religion in man's life as a more dynamic and practical mode of perfecting society rather than his misadventure into practical politics. "I can preach now, not merely make discussions on ethics and metaphysics. . . . I now need to know nothing but Jesus and him crucified."[25]

The establishment of Brook Farm in 1841 provided Brownson with a quiet, happy retreat from the warring classes of society. Founded under the leadership of his friend, George Ripley, Brook Farm was an experiment in cooperative living. A classless society, with no selfish competition, each member of it contributed the product of his labors to be enjoyed equally by all the members of the select community. Some of America's outstanding intellectuals of the nineteenth century were from time to time associated with it: Hawthorne, Alcott, Charles A. Dana, Margaret Fuller, Parker. While Brownson appeared to favor much of the social and intellectual camaraderie at Brook Farm, he was ill at ease with the Transcendentalism of his confreres. He was too realistic; the others, too idealistic. Brook Farm for him was a temporary escape from a divided society. Rather than live in so idealistic a clime, he returned to the reform of society, which most people regard as reality.

Refreshed from his experience at Brook Farm, and his bitterness after the election of 1840 now somewhat subsided, Brownson proceeded to look with a fresher insight into society. Writing now as a contributing editor of the *Democratic Review* he offered an essay on "The Present State of Society," which Russell Kirk has praised: "I do not know of anything published in the past several years quite so pertinent to our present discontents, more than a century after Brownson wrote this article."[26]

Commenting on Thomas Carlyle's book *Past and Present* in 1843, Brownson proceeds in "The Present State of Society" to offer his own evaluation of the state of society and the remedies for improving it. The abject misery and wretchedness of the working classes which Carlyle portrays in England can apply also to the United States. England may be the richest country in the world, but what does it benefit the poor who cannot find work? Newly invented machinery has caused economic dislocation. Overproduction has resulted in making "too many shirts to have a shirt to our back."[27] Likewise, "in this wealthy, charitable, industrious, Christian city of Boston . . . we have come . . . to our bread and soup society!"[28] The so-called "land of opportunity" affords no opportunity. Crime, vice, delinquency become the necessary means of the poor to acquire their daily bread. Brownson agrees with Carlyle in the pin-pointing of the cause for this sad state—men have substituted the worship of Mammon for the worship of God. Mournfully does Brownson describe the substitution:

> For the last three hundred years we have lost or been losing our faith in God, in heaven, in love, in justice, in eternity, and been acquiring faith only in human philosophies, in mere theories concerning supply and demand, wealth of nations, self-supporting, labor-saving governments; needing no virtue, wisdom, love, sacrifice, or heroism on the part of their managers; working out for us a new Eden, converting all the earth into an Eldorado land, and enabling us all to live in Eden Regained. We have left

behind us the living faith of the earlier ages; we have abandoned
our old notions of heaven and hell; and have come, as Carlyle
well has it, to place our heaven in success in money matters, and
to find the infinite terror men call hell, only in not succeeding
in making money. We have thus come—where we are.[29]

Brownson then challenges those who regard the industrialization of society as such an advance in the historical process over
the feudal Middle Ages characterized as a "dark" period of history. Businessmen in the Middle Ages, he observed, possessed
faith and a superior morality. Under the leadership of the
Church, the poor and defenseless were protected. The state was
not a means for the rich to hold sway over the masses but was
a guardian of humanity. Even in non-socio-economic fields, such
as philosophy, architecture, literature, the present affords little
rival for the thought and genius of the Middle Ages.[30]

Viewing what may be considered the four principal agents
responsible for the progress of modern society, Brownson insists
that these are the product of the "immense force accumulated
in the interior of man" during the so-called Dark Ages. First, the
art of war before the fifteenth century was the prerogative of
the noble class. The training and equipment of the warrior
prevented the poor peasant from becoming an efficient member
of the army. Kings, therefore, had to depend on their nobles to
such a degree that without their military support they were ineffective. The invention and use of firearms lessened the role
of the cavalry and placed greater emphasis on the infantry, into
which commoners could more readily be integrated. This change
in the art of war gave kings a lesser dependence on the nobility
and more use of the services of the commoners, whose status
now rose because of their employ in the service of kings. Even
the power of the Church was weakened, or at least neutralized,
by this shift in military power, as the people more naturally
rendered their requested loyalty to the service of the monarch.[31]

With the nobles now relieved of much of their role in military
service, they could preoccupy themselves more in letters and
thought, formerly the almost exclusive privilege of the clergy.
This trend paved the way for the study of the ancient Roman
and Greek classics, since the taking of Constantinople led to a
renewed interest in Greek scholarship. Absorption in the search-

ing mind of the Greeks replaced the rather complacent mind of faith so typical of the Church's influence in medieval thought. Education spread to more and more people but an immense class of superficial thinkers was created, one only too eager to embrace heathen literature, which by its nature Brownson regarded as lacking the strength and earnestness of Christian literature. In their superficiality the novices in the study of letters forgot that the church had already retained from the Roman and Greek classics that which was really of worth and consistent with the Christian faith. Nevertheless, the emphasis placed on the classics of antiquity led to a lessening of the Church's intellectual influence and, subsequently, to an order of thought favorable to the supremacy of the civil over the ecclesiastical. Civil governments became independent, kings were freed from their dependence on feudal nobles and the Church, and politics divorced from moral and religious doctrines and principles came into vogue—epitomized in the writings of Machiavelli. Where once a spiritual Church commanded and men obeyed, now a material state commands and even determines the faith of its people.[32]

The invention of printing has also aided in the lessening of the influence of the Church and the nobility of the Middle Ages. But its effects Brownson regards as not so good as generally upheld; for, in producing a great mass of readers, there has been fostered a spirit of proud individualism over the old spirit of humble submission.[33]

Brownson sees in the above causes of arrogant individualism in matters of faith, centralization of power in the hands of monarchs, the divorce of politics from morality, the setting of the stage for a new order in the wake of new land discoveries and trade routes, the start of industrial aggrandizement, and "the accumulation of treasures on earth, forgetful that moth and rust may corrupt and thieves break through and steal."[34] The industrial world saw visions of untold wealth. "The love of gold supplanted the love of God."[35] Pilgrimages were made not to the Holy Land but to the lands offering gold.

Since Mammon has taken the place of God, Brownson now calls for a re-evaluation of society. The arbitrary power of monarchs need not be feared—not the oppression of government, civil or ecclesiastical—but the present industrial order, which does not provide the worker with the work he needs to acquire

the necessities of life. To remedy the present state of society, we
need not go back to the feudalism of the Middle Ages. Firearms,
heathen literature, printing, and the new industrial order would
make it impossible even if it were desirable. But we should seek
to revive "in all its medieval force and activity the Christian
faith."[36] God's moral law must be brought back into political
chambers and into the business market places. He charges the
leaders of industry:

> If you govern industry only with a view to your own profit, to
> the profit of master-workers, we tell you that the little you
> contribute to build work-houses, and to furnish bread and soup,
> will not be held as a final discharge. If God has given you
> capacities to lead, it has been that you might be a blessing to
> those who want that capacity. God . . . will hold you responsible
> for the wise organization of industry and the just distribution of
> its fruits.[37]

In other writings Brownson continued his crusade for the respect of the workingman's rights, which he defined as "freedom
for each individual to act out his individuality, or to perform
his special function in the social body."[38] He further called on
government to aid the cause of the workingman: "We are no
believers in the sovereign virtue of free competition. . . . There
are times and cases when government is needed to control it,
to set bounds to it; when the government itself should take the
initiative, and assume the direction."[39] Mere political equality
does not suffice for the workingman as "universal suffrage does
not . . . give to every man equal ability to protect his own
rights and interests" while the capitalist reaps the profits and
strengthens his economic and political power.[40] With the industrial class gaining in power, a new feudalism is arising, an
industrial feudalism supplanting the military feudalism of the
Middle Ages. He sets forth this feudal transition as follows:

> Our industrial system is working gradually, but surely, the sub-
> jection of the great mass of the operative classes, and when our
> new lands shall have been exhausted, and the price of land
> become so high that the laboring man can no longer hope to be-
> come a proprietor . . . we shall find established all over the
> country an industrial feudalism, of which the military feudalism

of the middle ages was but a faint prelude. All is settling down into this new feudalism, and the whole legislation of the country, in relation to banks, tariffs and corporations generally, is rapidly hastening it.[41]

In a speech on social reform in the summer of 1844, Brownson pinpoints the sad effects of the new feudalism: gradual reducing of wages, placing labor in the same class as a commodity responsive to the fluctuating law of supply and demand; losing of jobs due to newly invented machinery; overproducing to meet competition and lower costs—all resulting in economic instability for the workingman now reduced virtually to a slave of industrial capitalism. How well Brownson penetrated into the socio-economic effects of the Industrial Revolution can be seen by his analysis of mass unemployment and the workingman's insecurity brought on by the booms and depressions of the business cycle:

There is no longer any certainty of the born worker obtaining always work whereby he can provide for the ordinary wants of a human being. . . . By our vicious method of distributing the products of labor, we destroy the possibility of keeping up an equilibrium between production and consumption. We create a surplus—that is, a surplus, not when we consider the wants of the people, but when we consider the state of the markets—and then must slacken our hands till the surplus is worked off. During this time, while we are working off the surplus, while the mills run short time, or stop altogether, the workingmen must want employment. The evil is inherent in the system.[42]

As the same problems exist substantially today for the workingman, as automation and foreign competition offer new challenges to industry, rightfully could Schlesinger say in praise of Brownson that he "observed the defects of capitalism with a sagacity possessed by few of his contemporaries."[43]

While Brownson wrote on the evils of industrial capitalism, his old friend George Ripley of Brook Farm fame had now become engaged in a new utopian socialist movement and was introducing it in his Transcendentalist community. Called Fourierism after its founder Charles Fourier, it believed in the essential holiness of human nature; evil in the world resulted only from causes extraneous to man. Brownson classified Fourierism as disguised Epicurianism—man's end is pleasure and happiness. Fourierism proposed to enable man to enjoy all his natural instincts and passions so that no evil will be experienced. To accomplish this purpose, Fourierism would organize families into the phalanx or townships; townships would be further organized into counties, counties into states, and finally the states into one grand harmonious association for the race.

The phalanx as the basic unit of society would be composed of some fifteen hundred to two thousand individuals who would be distributed into groups according to their natural aptitudes and interests, thus guaranteeing harmony in human nature. But Brownson rejected such an idealistic arrangement on the grounds that it ignores man's freedom. If man could not be perfectly satisfied in the garden of Eden, what assurance is there that he will not be tempted to sin in the phalanx? Furthermore, since Fourier sought to establish this society with a total indifference to all religious matters, the association lacked an organic principle to bind it together and sectarian controversies would arise to endanger the desired harmony among its members.[44]

Brownson insisted that the material goods of this earth could not guarantee complete happiness, for they never could satiate man's unending thirst for more and more material goods. Man's outlook must be other-worldly; he must subordinate material goods to spiritual goods. Fourierism confined its thoughts and affections to this life, with all appetites gratified; it was indifferent to spiritual concerns. Fourierism, therefore, appeared to Brownson as a theory based on false premises and as anti-Christian.

II *The Social Conservative*

The early 1840's were years of serious preoccupation with religion for Brownson. He embraced the Roman Catholic faith in 1844 and his intense study of the role of Christ as the redeemer of sinful man changed his point of view and emphasis even in his socio-economic thinking. Again he noted the religious basis as necessary for social reform: "The longer I live, the more I see of life, and the more I perceive of the complication of all questions, how one question runs into another, and no one can be answered as an isolated, independent question."[45] He then went to to ask the question, "With ignorant, depraved men, can you have a rightly organized society?"[46] The action of divine grace in man's interior life must, therefore, precede the struggle for social reform in man's exterior life.

With the acceptance of Roman Catholicism Brownson obtained a spiritual serenity. Instead of continuing his efforts for the reform of society, he accepted for the moment its *status quo*:

> This world is but an inn; we lodge in it but for a night, and what matters the inconvenience which we may be required to put up with? If we gain heaven it is nothing; and if we fail of heaven, the memory of it will be lost in the presence of an infinitely greater calamity.[47]
>
> . . . .
>
> So we need not trouble ourselves with philosophical, political, social or economic problems as such. Let us once acquire the virtues indispensable to salvation, and these problems will solve themselves, or cease to need solution.[48]

But Brownson was not long to remain in smug complacency in regard to socio-economic questions. He saw a need to discuss these questions from a Catholic point of view. Alarmed at the revolutionary upheavals of mid-nineteenth-century Europe and at the favorable acceptance of them by some American liberal journalists, he set out to demonstrate that these revolutions were not in the interests of the people as claimed. The leaders of these European revolutions he pictured as "real despots, savages, and butchers."[49] "A more God-forgetting and God-forsaken set of mortals it would be difficult to find, than the leaders of the European liberals."[50]

Conversion to Catholicism and the violence of the European liberals were factors in the transformation of Brownson from a vigorous radical, as exemplified in his views on "The Laboring Classes," to a high-minded conservatism. He himself admits this change:

> In my youth I was a wild radical, and sympathized with rebels wherever I found them,—unless rebels against the authority of the mob. I took for granted, that all old institutions are bad, and tend only to restrain the free spirit of man, and I looked upon every established government as necessarily tyrannical, and hostile to liberty. Whoever seeks to demolish old institutions, and to overthrow all fixed government, belongs, I said, to the party of progress, and is on the side of humanity.[51]

As a social and economic conservative Brownson analyzes the evils of socialism and writes for those who "little suspect what is fermenting in the heated brains of this nineteenth century."[52] Brownson rejects socialism because its essence lies in the assumption that man's good can be found in the natural order and cannot be attained by individual effort. He finds socialism particularly pernicious when veiled under the cloak of Christianity. A popular advocate of such a brand of socialism was found in France in the teachings of Abbé de La Mennais, whom Pope Gregory XVI had condemned. Brownson takes to task La Mennais' identity of socialism and Christianity, for the French writer claimed that Christ established on earth an order by which "millions were to be blessed with heaven, as well as hereafter."[53] But Brownson distinguishes, "*in* the new order and *by* it,—not out of it and independently of it."[54] The attempt of socialism to harmonize the interests of all with the interests of each places a restriction on individual initiative, resulting in enslaving man to nature and to the social and political order which the individual cannot control. This condition, Brownson points out, is contrary to the Christian doctrine of liberty; for Christ came to free man from bondage—to make him free to pursue good on a natural and supernatural level entirely independent of the world. "No one depends on nature or other men for the power to fulfill his destiny,—to gain the end for which he was intended."[55]

III *Nativism*

The rise of Nativism and the activities of the Know-Nothing Party occasioned a brilliant analysis of one of the most difficult social questions of nineteenth-century America. Alarmed at the rising influx of Catholic immigrants into this country, native-born Protestants organized themselves into societies to show concern about the new foreign influence. The Nativisits found it difficult to accept the illiteracy, the poverty, the dress of the immigrants. They feared the losing of the American standard of living because of the foreigners' ready acceptance of meager wages. Commenting on the appointment of Fenwick as bishop of Boston, the *Boston Recorder* warned Americans as follows: "So, it seems, the Pope of Rome sends over his high-sounding titles to this republican country, appointing and dismissing at pleasure.

Let this influence become general—let the Roman Catholic religion become the general religion of the land—and what will become of our boasted liberty and free institutions."[56]

Attempts were made to free Roman Catholics from the "idolatry of Popery" by distributing King James Bibles, setting up classes for the study of Protestantism, and sending invitations to attend Protestant services. The failure of these efforts to lure the Irish away from their religion only intensified the convictions of the Nativists.[57] Typical was the denunciation of Catholicism from the Protestant pulpit as the religion in which "all the evils and corruptions of idolatry and imposture have been condensed and wielded with infernal wisdom and malignity against the Gospel."[58]

Bigotry even led to the destruction of Catholic Church property, the most famous incident being the burning of the Ursuline Sisters' Convent in Charlestown, Massachusetts in 1834. The non-Catholic historian Billington concluded that only "class antipathies, religious jealousies and economic conditions could make possible such wanton destruction of property possible."[59]

In Brownson's writings on Nativism, he sought to dispel the Nativist prejudice by declaring the patriotic sentiment of the newly arrived immigrants. Yet he did so with such a remarkable insight into the feelings of the Nativists that some of his co-religionists wondered on whose side he stood. Writing as a native-born American, Brownson sees no necessity for any movement against foreigners who desire to adopt a new country. Since its discovery America has been regarded as an asylum for the downtrodden and persecuted of the world. People from different lands and cultures have risen above purely accidental distinctions to join themselves together in a nation bound by the principle that all men are to be judged by their personal worth. History shows immigrants to have fought for American freedom in wars and to have contributed to the economic expansion of the country.

The opposition of native Americans to foreigners is based on prejudice—a long-standing contempt of those of English descent for the Irish who form the bulk of the new immigrants. Furthermore, the Nativists are selective in their opposition to foreigners; it is only the Irish Catholics whom they resent and not Protestants from other European countries. Brownson refers to the

Constitution to demonstrate the un-Americanism of the Nativists, for the Constitution not merely tolerates but also guarantees to all men the free exercise of their religion. He seeks to allay the fears of the Nativists that Roman Catholics have a higher allegiance to a foreign power by pointing out the Catholic teaching on allegiance to civil authority and to country and that a republic can stand only as it rests upon the virtues of the people. He emphasizes the compatibility of Catholicism with American democracy and argues that for the Catholic Church,

> her chief concern is to fit men for beatitude, and this she can do under any or all forms of government. But the spirit she breathes into men, the graces she communicates, the dispositions she cultivates, and the virtues she produces, are such, that, while they render even arbitrary forms of government tolerable, fit a people for asserting and maintaining freedom.[60]

Brownson looked upon the Nativist movement with little apprehension in 1845; but, viewing its progress and intensity of activity against the Catholic foreigners, he was to write again on the subject in 1854.[61] He approaches the subject somewhat differently this time; he requests respect for native Americanism because the truest love of any man, after God, is for his country. He asks foreigners to appreciate the affection of Americans for their native land and the jealous attachment they have for its usages, manners, and customs. At the same time, he warns of the immigrants' motives of personal advantage and gain in coming to this country; and, while they may wish to adhere to their own customs, it is for them to conform to us rather than for us to conform to them. When these foreigners refuse to accept our traditions and even speak and write of undermining them, it is no wonder that they arouse the resentment of the native Americans. Brownson, therefore, justifies the indignation of the Nativists on this ground. Particularly with the Irish immigrant does he do so because a number of them had brought to this country their long-standing hostility to the English, who comprise at least three-fourths of the white population in the United States and more than any other European nationality are responsible for American institutions.

Yet, on the other hand, Brownson repudiates the native American party for its outward contradiction of the true American spirit. It opposes Catholic foreigners almost exclusively and on religious grounds denies them an opportunity for freedom, while professedly espousing religious liberty. The hostility of the native American toward Catholic foreigners and attempts to proselytize them have only served to compel them to resist any acculturation into American customs and even forced them to congregate as a distinct and separate people. Brownson, therefore, asks Americans to check the demogogical spirit in themselves and not to err in classifying foreigners as radicals when they themselves are exemplifying a radical spirit untrue to their own American institutions. In the gradual assimilation of the foreign into the native population with the passage of time, and in mutual forbearance, Brownson sees a solution to the problem.

In three articles of his *Quarterly Review* in the years 1854-55, Brownson deals with the Know-Nothing Party in the United States.[62] He brands the party as " a secret anti-Catholic organization throughout the Union, having some resemblance to the Orange lodges of Ireland."[63] As a party it represents, he feels, a small segment of Americans, and Catholics should resist any inclination to associate them with "the large class of respectable non-Catholics who love their country more than they hate popery."[64] Brownson states that Catholics should strive to indicate their allegiance to their newly adopted country and thereby demonstrate the compatibility of Roman Catholicism with democratic institutions. They may have to forsake many of their cherished foreign traditions but never their religion; for an unnecessary clinging to the former could indicate the desire to segregate themselves into social, economic, and even political divisions, while maintaining their religious beliefs is an avowed American principle of religious freedom. He again emphasized in these articles some previously written views on the past and potential contribution of foreigners to this country and the need for understanding on the part of native Americans.

Brownson's treatment of the Nativist controversy manifests a keen appreciation of the process of acculturation that has been taking place in our country since its founding. Acculturation cannot take place overnight; it is a gradual process. Acculturation seeks a blending of cultures, not a destruction of them. When assured of a blending, foreigners become more receptive to the process of acculturation. Acculturation condones the holding on to cherished traditions even while it requires an allegiance to a new country, with its new customs, usages, and manners. Unity in diversity has been an ideal of American democratic life, and Brownson stands as one of those Americans who, in the nineteenth century at a crucial point of the country's population expansion, contributed to the process of acculturation of foreign Catholics into the country of their adoption.

An example of Brownson's insight into the feelings of the Nativists and the hesitancy of Catholics to acculturate themselves into American life can be seen in his articles on Catholic education.[65] The Roman Catholic hierarchy with its strong stand for a Catholic school in every parish did not welcome such views; but these views do demonstrate Brownson's objectivity in analyzing the Nativist problem. He cites the need for a thorough Catholic education in subject matter and over-all religious spirit. Such an education could only be achieved in a Catholic school. But at the same time he points out that the Catholic schools of the day "are taught chiefly by foreigners, or, if not by foreigners, at least by those whose sympathies and connections, tastes and habits are un-American."[66] He agreed to the urgency of establishing Catholic schools because of the anti-Catholicism in the public school textbooks and in the Protestant spirit of the teachers.[67] However, he regarded the establishment of Catholic parochial schools as premature; they were not quite ready to measure up to the standards of instruction and qualifications of the teachers in the public schools. He therefore urged parents to send their children to public schools when these were evidently superior.

Brownson, however, did not advise the elimination of Catholic parochial schools. Such a position he acknowledged as futile since the hierarchy had made them a "fixed fact." But Catholic education needed a new perspective. It could not produce the effective American Catholic by being subservient to foreign culture, however orthodox it might be regarded from the standpoint of religion. Living in a heterodox culture postulated an education to cope with the problems this type of culture engendered. With a wholesale conversion of America to Roman Catholicism not imminent in any foreseeable future, Catholic youths would have to be trained to meet the needs of the American society in which they lived and not for "taking refuge in the cloister, in an exclusive or exaggerated asceticism."[68] Such words may not have been, and still would not be, pleasing to the American hierarchy, but they were a partial assurance to the Nativists questioning whether Roman Catholic immigrants and their children could make any worth-while contribution to a land not of their birth.

IV *Slavery*

Brownson enjoyed no reputation for being on the side of the majority on many issues. Particularly in the matter of slavery is he found holding a position unexpected of a Northerner and of a Roman Catholic.

It was during the financial struggle of the late 1830's that he first expressed views on the subject of slavery. Noticing a common lot between the helplessness of the Northern workingmen at the mercy of the industrial capitalist and the Southern cotton picker at the hands of the plantation owner, Brownson took on more of the views of a Southerner than of a Northerner. He acknowledged slavery as an evil, but he advised the Abolitionists that "reformers should war against systems, not against men."[69] He regarded this social problem as reflecting the general tone of society rather than as a personal moral problem. "Slavery," he insisted, "is not an individual, but a social institution, and society, not the individual conscience, is responsible for it."[70]

What of the wretched working and living conditions of the laborers in the North? The answer to this question he relegated to the Abolitionists and asked that they attend to their obligation of first cleaning up their own homes in the North before casting the stone of guilt on Southerners; for Brownson made no distinction between the evils of capitalism and those of slavery.[71] The social and working conditions of the Northern laborers were no better than those of the Southern slaves: "As to actual freedom one has just about as much as the other."[72] In an address to a group of college students he delineated the fallacy of the Northerner's objections to slavery in the South:

> You of the South consist of freemen and slaves, of gentle and simple, and so do we of the North. In both sections we find at bottom the same distinction of classes, though while you have the manliness to avow it, we have the art to disguise it from the careless observer, under the drapery of fine names. You call your

slaves by their proper name, and while you impose upon them the duties of slaves, you relieve them from the cares and burdens of freemen; we call our slaves freemen, and impose upon them the labors and burdens of slavery, while we secure to them none of the advantages of freedom. The only advantage we can claim over you is, that our slaves being of the same race and color with our freemen, are individually less hopelessly slaves than yours. The class is as permanent with us as with you; but individuals of the class may more easily escape from it, and rise in their own persons or in their children to the class of freemen. But on the other hand, if our slaves are under certain aspects less slaves than yours, our freemen are less free than yours.[73]

To defeat the Whigs, whom he identified as the party of big business and as against the workingman, Brownson called upon the workers of the North to join with the slaveholders of the South. This was obviously a peculiar twist of reasoning but only in such a coalition could he see the eventual defeat of Whig policies.[74]

But how did Brownson view slavery in itself? Expressing no sympathy with the Abolitionists, he set forth a view not fully consonant with the Catholic position on the doctrine of man's equality:

Man, we are ready to maintain, may have property in man, a valid right to the services of his slave,—though no dominion over his soul; slavery is *malum in se* and in no case justifiable; there is nothing in slavery that necessarily prevents the slaveholder from being a true and pious Christian; and where the master is a true Christian, and takes care that his people are instructed and brought up in the true Christian faith and worship, slavery is tolerable, and for negroes, perhaps, even more than tolerable.[75]

Brownson even regarded any immediate emancipation as "the greatest disservice" to the slaves, because they would be left to take care of themselves at a time when they were not yet ready for such a step.[76] Thus, he maintained that slavery was a matter for each state to decide and not a concern of the federal government. A new state seeking admission to the Union should not, therefore, be refused admittance because it believed in slavery, in as much as states presently members have such a right.[77]

But, since slavery became a national problem to the point of civil war, Brownson had to modify his position. He did not think that the South would ever secede from the Union and engage in war. Still preferring slavery to be decided on a local level with efforts for emancipation on a gradual scale, he now called for the preservation of the Union and for the defeat of the South.[78] The Civil War created for Brownson an uncompromising choice: slavery or no slavery. With his previous compromising position no longer tenable, he chose no slavery and delineated the mockery that slavery held for a democracy that believes in the doctrine of the Christian equality of man: "The advance of freedom is the destruction of slavery. We can, then, secure an open field for freedom, and prevent the slave interest from domineering, only by abolishing it, and recognizing the slaves as free. The republic to subsist and flourish must either be all free or all slave."[79]

Brownson devoted an entire article in the *Quarterly Review* on the teaching of the Catholic Church on slavery.[80] He thereby justified his previous position by pointing out that the Church does not teach that slavery is always, everywhere, and under all circumstances, a sin for the individual slaveholder. Social necessity could justify slavery, such as slaves being inherited from parents or the situation being such that slavery would be a better condition than freedom. But he firmly upheld the Church's condemnation of chattel slavery, the complete disregarding of a slave as a human person with God-given rights of freedom. He branded slavery in the Southern states as chattel slavery. In advocating the Northern cause, he made use of the moral arguments resorted to when he had espoused the Southern cause.

Yet, while defending the Union's cause in the war, Brownson clearly pointed out that the Civil War ought not to be considered a war against Southern society and the Southern people. Rather the Civil War could find justification only "in vindication of national integrity . . . in defence of government, of authority, and the supremacy of law."[81] Those who sought to make the South like New England he considered to be following a false philanthropy, characteristic of the Puritan who by nature wishes to impose his will on others without waiting patiently for the practical effects of reform as the true law of progress requires. In defense of Southern society he regards its leaders as naturally superior; they are more deliberate, more patient, and more enduring than Northern leaders. Furthermore, agricultural pursuits serve broader and more permanent interests of the nation, while trade and manufacturing, due to the instability of the money markets, frequently bring about changes of leadership; and the rich of today become the poor of tomorrow. Brownson wanted the North to guarantee that the Southern states would enjoy, upon the successful completion of the war, all rights of self-government with no attempt on the part of the North to revolutionize Southern society according to Northern ideas. What effect on post-Civil War relations between the North and South would these words of Brownson have had if American leaders had attended to them? "We wish to see the free-labor system substituted for the slave-labor system, but beyond that we have no wish to exchange or modify society and would rather approach northern society to it, than it to northern society."[82]

When Brownson became convinced that the Union had to be preserved at whatever cost, he spared no criticism of those who might question whether slavery was the main and basic issue of the conflict. Such a stand brought him into open conflict with Archbishop John Hughes of New York. Hughes had written to Simon Cameron, the Secretary of War, as follows:

> There is being insinuated in this part of the country an idea to the effect that the purpose of the war is the abolition of slavery in the South. If that idea should prevail among a certain class, it would make the business of recruiting slack indeed. The Catholics, so far as I know, whether of native or foreign birth, are willing to fight to the death for the support of the constitution, the Government, and the laws of the country. But if it should be understood that, with or without knowing it, they are to fight for the abolition of slavery then, indeed, they will turn away in disgust from the discharge of what would otherwise be a patriotic duty.[83]

Archbishop Hughes, moreover, was reputed to have written an article in the *Metropolitan Record,* the official organ of his diocese, on October 12, 1861, stating these same views. Brownson immediately branded Hughes's views as pro-slavery and as in direct contradiction of the Church's position on slavery.[84] Where Hughes wanted to remove slavery as a mere political issue in the Civil War, Brownson regarded slavery as the very *raison d'être* of the war: it was being fought for either destroying or continuing slavery, and no choice was permitted. The abolition of slavery and the preservation of the Union were one and the same thing. He rebuked his co-religionists who intimated that

> slavery and Catholicity are the only two conservative institutions in the country, and that to strengthen the slaveholding power would be to strengthen the Catholic Church. . . . In regard to civilization and the future prosperity of our religion on this continent, an anti-slavery Protestant is worth more than a pro-slavery Catholic.[85]

To the leaders of the Union, Brownson urged a quicker and firmer prosecution of the war. He opposed any compromise with any of the Southern states on readmittance to the Union. He urged a speedy, crushing defeat of the rebellion, with the government no longer pursuing a conciliatory policy and employing only timid and halfway measures.[86] He recommended striking the enemy at his weakest and sorest points. President Lincoln was not spared from criticism, since in 1862 he had not yet issued the Emancipation Proclamation. Brownson even suggested that he resign from the presidency.[87]

The main target of his criticism of the conduct of the Civil War became Secretary of State William H. Seward, whom he regarded as the author of the Lincoln administration's war policies. In October, 1862, Brownson pictured Seward as lacking "nerve, back-bone, high courage, and firm and generous resolve. His faculties avail him least when the danger he tries to meet is greatest."[88] In the hope of being in a position to bring a firmer prosecution of the war, Brownson accepted the Republican nomination for the United States House of Representatives in the third district of New Jersey and spoke extensively throughout the entire district. Political strategists felt that Brownson could gain the support of enough Catholic Democrats in a normally Democratic district to elect a Republican; but he was convincingly defeated by his opponent, William G. Steele, in the November election.

Dedication to the cause of the Union's victory, however, kept Brownson from discouragement; and he continued working for the Union in his lectures and writings. Still regarding Lincoln as unqualified for the presidency, he nevertheless announced support for his re-election in January, 1864. But the radicals in the Republican party were easily able to change Brownson's weak acceptance of Lincoln and urged him to participate in an anti-Lincoln movement. In April, 1864, Brownson voiced his opposition to Lincoln and called for the nomination of Salmon P. Chase, who declined any offer to run for President. So Brownson expressed preference for General John C. Frémont, who accepted Brownson's support in his efforts to defeat Lincoln. But in September, Frémont withdrew from the presidential race.[89] Brownson now remained committed against Lincoln and had no candidate of his own to support. His *Review* likewise was left without support, having lost most of its Catholic subscribers and political sympathizers. Writing in the summer of the next year, he acknowledged defeat: "My Review died of Fremont. Had I not supported the Pathfinder, or had he not withdrawn and left me in the lurch, I should have continued it, and I hope to be able yet to resume it. I stopped it because I had sacrificed my position, and had no party to fall back upon."[90]

Whether the positions taken by Brownson on slavery can be agreed with or not is a matter of opinion. Upon one fact all can agree: When Brownson's mind became set on a particular view or course of action, he pursued it with all his energies and persuasion as a writer. He first opposed the Northern Abolitionists because they condemned slavery in the South and permitted industrial servitude in the factories of the North—a stand taken after the war by many of the North as the cry arose to free the wage slaves. With equal vigor, however, Brownson opposed the South for secession and fought with the North for a quick and successful preservation of the Union; to achieve this objective, slavery had to be abolished.

CHAPTER 3

The Political Philosopher

BELIEF in the perfectibility of human nature lies at the very foundation of Brownson's political thought. In his religious thinking he veered from the extreme position of man's total depravity as taught by Calvin to the more hopeful belief in man's essential goodness. As a Christian social reformer he repeatedly stressed the betterment of man's earthly lot by moral reform. His work with the Society for Christian Union and Progress is a living example of devotion to the cause of the workingman. Genuine freedom under God for the governed and the governing becomes the motif of his political reasoning, even as he progresses from radicalism to conservatism.

I *The Political Radical*

Concerned with bettering the lot of the workingman, Brownson associated himself with the Workingman's Party, started in Philadelphia in 1828 and a year later in New York. The party's purpose was to gain control of the political power in the state and thereby put into effect the Owen-Wright theory of education, a program of "state guardianship," by which the state would control the educational training of all children beginning at two years of age. As editor of the Genesee *Republican and Herald of Reform,* published at Leroy, New York, Brownson staunchly defended the proposed theory of education. He resisted, however, the more radical path of Thomas Skidmore in the advocacy of agrarianism with equal division of property among all. But the workingmen found little practical value in these radical measures of either education or agrarianism; they fought instead for higher wages and for a working day of ten hours.

By nature an independent thinker, Brownson found it difficult to be a party man. He acknowledged a visionary fascination for the Owen-Wright proposals, but never felt deeply convinced of their value. He expressed fear of a program that would diminish parental authority over children and he could see that the state school would turn out only "well-trained animals."[1] What, therefore, led Brownson to associate himself with such radicalism? As a firm believer in the strength of unified forces, he hoped that a laborer's party might effect political action. But only a few months' experience was required to convince him that working-men are not sufficiently numerous nor strong enough to wield political power. The forces of capital possessed a wall too impregnable for the workingmen to break down: "Money commands the supplies, and can hold out longer than they who have nothing but their manhood. It can starve them into submission."[2] Brownson felt that, rather than direct his efforts to the working-men as a separate class, he could achieve far more effective results if he could induce all classes of society to cooperate in ameliorating the workingmen's plight.

Up to 1837, therefore, Brownson restricted himself to preaching social reform, at one time emphasizing individual moral reform and at other times placing more emphasis on social reform as a means to ameliorate conditions conducive for individual reform.[3] Convinced that the Whig Party was dominated by the moneyed class, he associated himself with the Democratic Party as the party of the common man. To aid the election of Van Buren over Harrison in 1840, he wrote the essays, "The Laboring Classes." He busied himself with writings on the economic policies of the parties and urged the people to support the Democrats as the party of the people. Described in the previous chapter, these articles and views of Brownson even became issues in the campaign. But the results of the election of that year proved his practical political venture one of the most discouraging periods in his life. With the Whigs' trouncing victory over the party of the people, Brownson asked himself if the people really cared for their interests. He lost faith in the people as the guardians of their own rights:

What I saw served to dispel my democratic illusions, to break the idol I had worshipped, and shook to its foundation my belief in the divinity of the people, or in their will as the expression of eternal justice. I saw that they could easily be duped, easily made victims of the designing, and carried away by an irresistible passion in the wrong as easily as in the right. . . . I ceased henceforth to believe in democracy.[4]

Brownson did not abandon the Democratic Party but sought to make it "more conservative, and to convince its leaders that the people as the state need governing no less than the people as individuals."[5] His political tone shifted, therefore, from that of "an impractical radical" to that of "political conservatism."[6] He, furthermore, subsequently began a revision of his political thinking and wrote articles of penetrating analysis, for he had come to the firm belief that "political theories must be tested not by their abstract beauty and excellence, but by their practical operations, the people being taken just as they are."[7]

II *Political Conservative*

While actively advocating radical social reforms, Brownson did not in his political writings demonstrate the same radical tendencies, due most likely to the fact that he did not set down in writing his thoughts on political philosophy while he was engaged in radical social movements. When he began an elaboration and synthesis of thoughts on the philosophy of government, he assumed a conservative tone; and, as a result, his views on most political questions continued unaltered through later writings.[8]

Among his first articles in the field of political thought is an essay entitled "Democracy" for the *Boston Quarterly Review* in January, 1838. In this essay he begins by a clarification of the term *democracy,* offering a philosophical analysis of the term rather than the more common views of democracy as government in which the people are ultimately responsible for the laws. He examines democracy as the name of a great social and political doctrine seeking to advance the masses to a better social condition.

Proceeding to the assertion that democracy is considered as the sovereignty of the people, Brownson points out the fallacy of such a belief: "If so, the people, taken collectively, are the absolute master of every man taken individually. Every man, as a man, then, is an absolute slave."[9] Democracy so viewed is in theory another form of absolutism, with the people instead of a king or an aristocracy exercising all the power over an individual. He continues in his exposition of the fallacy of the people's sovereignty when a democratic form of government requires all questions to be decided by a majority of the people. Sovereignty, then, passes from the people to the ruling majority; and "if the majority have the absolute right to govern, it is the absolute duty of the minority to obey."[10] The minority, which would become disfranchised and be placed at the mercy of the majority, would be in no better position than under an absolute monarchy or the most lawless aristocracy.

Who or what is sovereign in government? The answer to this question is the key to Brownson's philosophical analysis of democracy. The absolute sovereign is above the individual, king, nobles, and the people. "The absolute sovereign is justice, the sovereign of sovereigns, the king of kings, lord of lords, the supreme law of the people, and of the individual."[11] Two years earlier he had written on the nature of justice: "We make justice paramount to the popular will and acknowledge allegiance to the popular will only so far as it is in harmony with our convictions of the Just."[12] Elaborating further on justice, he identifies justice with God—not in the sense of the theocrat who makes the priesthood the symbol of sovereignty and the authoritative expounder of its decrees, but in the truly democratic sense, which makes justice known by "the universal reason which is ever shining in the human soul, and in making the people in a few instances, and the individual in all the rest, the only authoritative expounders of its decrees."[13]

Democracy so understood becomes for Brownson the doctrine of true liberty. Man is free to do whatever is just and not free to do what is unjust, as God's immutable laws have decreed. Democracy recognizes rights and duties for the state as well as for individuals. On both theoretical and operational levels there necessarily arises the problem of knowing where the rights and duties of the individual begin and where those of the state end, and vice versa. Defining the exact point of the beginning and end of these rights and duties for the individual and the state Brownson classifies as "the great political problem of our epoch."[14] To the moralist and politician alike he delegates this problem as a mission to guide man's future, and he states it in these words: "the conciliation of the individual with social, and of social with individual rights and the subordination of all social and individual action to the laws of justice, the law of nature or the law of God."[15]

Referring to the American constitutional form of government, Brownson stresses the fact that a higher force is the guarantee of the rights of individuals, rights which existed prior to any Constitution or Bill of Rights. Otherwise, the rights enumerated by these documents merely express the will of the majority and exist at the majority's discretion. Rights are not grants; documents are not needed to make rights legitimate: "Right and wrong, for governments, individuals, and societies, for cities and citizens, are eternal and immutable."[16] Man has rights by virtue of his human nature. Granted that Brownson was merely reiterating the political, Lockean concepts of the first settlers of America and of the founding fathers, Schlesinger referred to Brownson's statement of principles on democracy as a "novelty" for American thinking on government in 1838.[17]

With a loss of faith in the "intelligence of the people" because of their voting in the 1840 election, Brownson showed a more marked trend toward conservatism. Reflecting an Aristotelian influence, Brownson began a systematic exposition of his political philosophy in the *Boston Quarterly Review* in 1842.[18] Man, he reasoned, must live in society. If he were to live alone, he could not provide for himself all that he needs to live according to his nature. For orderly living in society, government is needed as the custodian of the common good. He views government not as a mere necessary evil to prevent the encroachment of one individual upon another or encroachment by various groups. Brownson regards the role of government more positively: its role was to labor for social progress and well-being, to maintain individual liberty, and to develop the manifold resources of a country for its people. It need not be any special type of government that can achieve these ends. Form of government in itself is merely a means to an end: "One form of government in itself is no more just and equitable than another, and no more obligatory upon a people. That form is best for a people, which in its practical workings best realizes the true end of government."[19]

Still maintaining his anti-Whig views, Brownson points out that, although the American government has declared all men to be equal in theory, the people in fact are nearly as unequal as in countries not classified as democracies. Property, for example, has not become more equally diffused but more concentrated in the hands of a few. Government, moreover, has legislated in favor of the interests of the moneyed classes. Theoretically, the government has vouchsafed protection of the natural liberty of individuals; *de facto* government has destroyed it by legislating for special interests. Nor is Brownson impressed by the argument of majority rule—this argument he believes is effective only if economic equality exists. Minority rights are still at the mercy of the majority. He presents to its advocates this shattering argument:

> Our democratic theorists . . . tell us the voice of the people is the voice of God; that what the people will is for the good of the whole; but however this may be in some refined transcendental sense, in practice the will of the people is the will of that interest in the community, which is able to command a majority, and the voice of the people is the voice of that interest.[20]

How can the rights and interests of the minorities in a constitutional government be safeguarded? Brownson proposes an effective veto on power. The methods of vetoing legislation as provided by the separation of powers in American government he deems inadequate, for usually both the executive and legislative branches of the government reflect the interests of the ruling majority. It is the states, reflecting the diverse economic interests of the nation—industrial, agricultural, commercial—that represent the economic division of the nation. Each state, therefore, as an entity, should possess the veto. Veto power then becomes not an artificial mechanism of the constitution but a natural implement of it. Legislation binding all would be effected only with the concurring majorities of the states.[21]

In proposing the concurring majorities as a natural veto power to protect minority interests, Brownson mirrored the thought of John C. Calhoun as expressed in the *Disquisition on Government*. This parallel was no mere chance. Brownson was an admirer and friend of Calhoun, having supported him in 1824.

Both were advocates of States' rights and of the same financial policies for the country. In 1839 Calhoun wrote Brownson: "I am moving towards a single end, to bring back the government, as far as constitutional measures are concerned, to where it commenced."[22] They had discussed with each other the system of concurring majorities and were convinced that such a system would protect the rights of minority interests.[23]

In typical Brownsonian fashion he stood alone among his fellow New Englanders in support of Calhoun's doctrine. It was a logical step to proceed to the defense of slavery, as he did, from the consideration of the economic interests of the states; for the South found in the doctrine of concurring majorities one of its strongest arguments to support slavery as an economic institution required for its very survival. But neither Brownson nor Calhoun carried the doctrine of concurring majorities to its logical conclusion. Were there not within each state economic divisions? No state then, and much more so now, was purely industrial, agricultural, or commercial. Each state would have its own problems of solving such conflicting interests. How could a state possibly act as a unit to express its true economic position?

In writing, however, against the Abolitionists who sought a quick emancipation of the slaves in the South, Brownson chooses to praise the strong individuality of the South. He sees in the Southern planter a sort of petty sovereign, and he lays stress on the importance of the individual; whereas he notes that the North, subservient to business interests, constantly hands over to the government more centralized power. The individual in the North becomes "a mere fraction of the body politic," as the tendency is to merge the individual in the state.[24] As the lord of his plantation, the Southerner does not lose his individuality; he is instead a jealous guardian of his rights as a man and not too eager to surrender them to the state. Brownson acknowledges that the Southerner did not at the time regard slaves as enjoying the same natural rights, but he did feel that with the passage of time the Southern planter would earnestly secure and defend the rights of Negroes when he no longer regarded himself as in danger from the Northern tendency to centralization.

In relegating too much power to the federal government, the individual finds himself more and more away from the reins of government—thousands of miles away in some cases. He thus begins to regard his part in the government as comparatively insignificant, even loses his individuality as he becomes more lost in the masses. The doctrine of state rights keeps the government closer to the individual, encourages more active participation in local affairs, and keeps the individual more alert and sensitive to the government's restricting of individual rights.[25]

As Brownson formulated his political philosophy from 1843 in the *Democratic Review,* his loss of faith in the people becomes even more apparent. "Mentioning this 1840, we must say that it marks an epoch in *our* political and social doctrines. The famous election of that year wrought a much greater revolution in us than in the government."[26] He no longer accepted the democratic view expressed in the words, "the intelligence of the people." Nor could he see the future of freedom being secured through a greater extension of popular suffrage. He objected to the definition of democracy as the sovereignty of the people: "The *people* in a legal or political sense, properly speaking, have no existence, no entity, therefore no rights, no sovereignty, save when organized into a body politic."[27] The view that democracy is a form of government, he believes, is erroneous; democracy should be viewed as a principle rather than as a form. A true democrat seeks the freedom and progress of all men, which will not be secured by "loose radicalism" with regard to popular sovereignty and by the "demogogical boasts of the virtue and intelligence of the people."[28]

Because of these views Brownson was called undemocratic and was charged with forsaking the cause of the Democratic Party in working for the people's interests. He was even accused of turning Whig. Although the de-emphasis on the people's power in government was true, it was not a loss of faith in democratic institutions that characterized Brownson at this time. He preferred to regard democracy more as an end rather than as a means. A re-evaluation of America's political thought was needed, and this he proceeded to make. The 1840's was a period of intellectual revolution in all of Brownson's thinking. He was becoming less radical and more conservative in his theological, socio-economic, and political thinking. He was less the idealist of youth and more the realist of adulthood. Evolutionary progress was more feasible than sweeping changes. He wrote: "We do not thus in age forget the dreams of our youth. . . . As we grow older, sadder, and wiser, and pass from idealists to realists, we . . . learn that the only true way of carrying the race forward is through its existing institutions."[29]

In offering to the readers of the *Democratic Review* in 1843 three articles on the "Origin and Ground of Government," his purpose was to present a scientific exposition of politics, a project that he felt had not yet been adequately performed in the United States and that was a need for American politicians who "disregard questions pertaining to the origin and purpose of the state as mere abstractions and altogether beneath the notice of the wise, practical statesman."[30]

In these essays, Brownson rejects the social compact theory of government, even though it may have been a theory of much influence upon the founding fathers. Such a theory, based on the assumption that government has and can have no just powers but those derived from the consent of the governed, resolves all government into self-government with no distinction between the governing and the governed, resulting in the situation where "the restrained is the restrainer, the guided is the guide, the directed director."[31] Accepting the compact theory without qualification becomes a *reductio ad absurdum*: "If the law controls the people, how can the people, as subject to the law, be the force that imposes the law?"[32]

Can government acquire its power from the majority of the governed? The concept of majority rule, a topic previously dealt with by Brownson, becomes another important theory that he examines in these articles. Again he emphasizes this fallacy in American political thought, for the minority remains at the mercy of the majority. Such a theory even destroys the foundation of morality, for it renders the distinction between right and wrong not fixed and eternal but arbitrary and variable, truly permitting "might to make right." Majority rule should be classified as a "mere *civil* regulation" and not as a natural right or as an ordinance of God.[33]

For Brownson, all power is of God; and no government of mere human origin is or ever can be legitimate. Reasoning from the principles of Christian philosophy, he argues that all being must have its origin in a first being, which is called God, the source of all being. From man's freedom given to him by God, man makes the practical arrangements determining his civil rulers, and this choice of man is an expression of the divine will. Brownson's thinking as to the origin of government is a *via media* between the divine right of kings and the popular-sovereignty theories. He actually proposes a theocratic-democratic position, for he acknowledges the divine origin of government with rulers chosen by the free will of man.[34] But such a notion of the origin of government is not Brownson's alone. The historian Bancroft so viewed it also, for he defined democracy as "eternal justice ruling through the people"; to him, eternal justice and the will of God were synonymous.[35]

Application of Brownson's ideas is made to the American form of government, and it leads Brownson to reject the American system as a representative democracy. Not only is such a government administered by the people but their will, however expressed, is considered the supreme law. He prefers identifying the American government as a constitutional republic: "a government in which power is held as a trust from the commonwealth, to be exercised for the public good, according to a prescribed law, whether actually exercised by one man called king or emperor, by the few called the nobility or aristocracy, or by the many, called the people."[36] In a democracy the majority can enact any law it deems expedient for its own interests, but in a constitutional republic the majority is held in check by the constitution representing the will of the people as a whole. Guaranteed in this constitution are the equal rights of all citizens as God has bestowed them upon man, and these a majority of citizens, however large, can never take away.

Brownson, in setting forth the American government as a constitutional republic, actually reiterated one of the best classic treatments of the American system: that contained in *The Federalist* of Hamilton, Madison, and Jay. He may have been on the side of political orthodoxy, but his readers were under the impression that he nurtured undemocratic ideas. The editor of the *Democratic Review*, J. L. O'Sullivan, prefaced one of Brownson's articles in 1843 with an apology for such views on the role of the people in the American government. Brownson's analysis of the evils in American society led to his preferring some of the features of feudalism to industrial capitalism.[37] Readers of his articles on government sent complaints to the editor inquiring about Brownson's verbosity and rather perplexing reasoning, which they classified as a "fine specimen of transcendental nonsense."[38] Brownson even gave some acknowledgment to his readers' complaints when he replied: "However unmeaning it may be to them, it has meaning to me, and I know very well what I mean by it: by what phraseology, or whether any phraseology will suffice to communicate my meaning to their minds, I own, I am at some loss to determine."[39]

But the rising disapproval of the articles on government led O'Sullivan to request Brownson's withdrawing his services from the periodical and then to disassociate himself from any of Brownson's views.[40] Still determined to set forth the views of which he was convinced, Brownson revived the *Boston Quarterly*, which he had edited, and called it *Brownson's Quarterly Review;* it first appeared in January, 1844.

Brownson's withdrawal from the *Democratic Review* also afforded the opportunity to clarify his stand in practical politics. He could more easily align himself now with the Southern Democrats instead of with the Northern Democrats. His admiration for Calhoun's political thought was to be extended to the putting of these ideas into the realm of practical politics. In October, 1841, Calhoun had suggested to Brownson his interest in the presidential nomination of 1844.[41] An offer to edit a pro-Calhoun paper in New York in 1843 was made but later revoked because of the lack of funds.[42] Not having much regard for Van Buren who had charged that his essays on "The Laboring Classes" were a principal cause of his defeat in 1840, Brownson set out to oppose him. In the first issue of *Brownson's Quarterly Review* he classified the re-election of Van Buren as "a most serious public calamity."[43] He spared no adjective in describing Van Buren's unfitness to acquire the office to which the American people had once before refused to re-elect him.

While one article of the first issue of his *Quarterly* sought to discredit Van Buren, another article pleaded for the nomination of Calhoun as an eminently practical statesman."[44] All the praise heaped on Calhoun's political career can be summarized in the words: "The presidential chair may receive new lustre and dignity from him; to him it can give none."[45]

But again Brownson had to chalk up a defeat in practical politics. To Brownson's dismay Calhoun asked to be withdrawn from the race for the presidential nomination at the Baltimore convention. Brownson wrote an article in April, 1844, asking for reconsideration on the part of Calhoun and his political associates.[46] He argued a now-or-never possibility of his being elected President, holding that to wait for a more opportune time in 1848 would be too late for the country's welfare. But Calhoun remained adamant in his decision.

Although Calhoun was removed from the presidential race, Brownson did find occasion to rejoice when the Democrats rejected Van Buren at their convention and nominated James K. Polk. Brownson promised his support for Polk and deemed him an able, irreproachable gentleman of considerable political experience.[47] He further claimed that he could campaign "with heart" for Polk, but he still wanted his own stand on political issues clarified. He classified himself as in agreement, however, more with the Whigs "in many of the abstract principles of government" than with his fellow Democrats; for with the Whigs he shared the belief in a stronger constitutional republic than in representative democracy. But "as the party of modern feudalism, . . . there is not one of their distinctive measures but will tend directly and with fatal force to consolidate the power of the industrial lords, and to reduce the operative classes to a state of virtual serfage."[48] He did not feel that the present leaders of the Democratic Party were doing all that they could for the interests of all classes, yet he had no hope at all that the Whigs would care to do anything.

During the election campaign of 1844, although he backed the Democratic candidate, Brownson viewed himself more in the role of a "censor of both parties than a partisan of either."[49] But he did take issue with Polk on the matter of the tariff because he felt the Democratic position discriminated in favor of home industry and so, in lessening the ability of the foreigner to sell to us, it likewise lessened his ability to buy from us.[50] He nevertheless rejoiced in Polk's victory and desired that his disagreement on the tariff issue not be taken as a sign of his dissenting from the Democrats and turning Whig but of his being no slavish adherent to a party and free to stress principles rather than parties: "It is better to be defeated with our principles than to succeed without them."[51]

The year 1844 marked his conversion to Roman Catholicism, and Brownson subsequently became more absorbed with theological questions than with politics. Most of his Protestant readers withdrew their subscriptions from the *Quarterly Review;* and, while it did gain new subscribers among Catholics, the periodical, for several years, gradually declined in number of subscriptions.

Although Brownson, upon joining the Catholic Church, became primarily concerned with theological questions in the hope of acquiring "the virtue indispensable to salvation," he nevertheless insisted on the role of religion in advancing a nation. In an essay on "National Greatness," he emphasized individual greatness as the *sine qua non* of a country's greatness, and he advocated that the individual be judged by his love of God and his keeping of the Commandments.[52] Material wealth should be subordinated to the attainment of a higher goal, man's supernatural destiny: "No man is great but as he is good, but as he lives in the order of grace, and loves God above all things and with his whole heart and soul, and his neighbour as himself in and for the sake of God."[53] He, therefore, challenged the American people to live individually, and hence collectively, by the maxims of the Gospel and to seek to solve the political and socio-economic questions of the day in the Christian spirit of brotherly concern for the rights of all.

Brownson found reason to give approbation to the views of the French writer, Count Joseph de Maistre, because they condemned those who sought to remove God from political constitutions and to advocate liberty on principles which logically put man in the place of God. Americans would find special value in such a consideration since too many of them had leaned too heavily on the naturalistic conceptions of government as espoused by Hobbes, Locke, Rousseau, and Paine—men who had a strong tendency to forget that Divine Providence had something to do with the formation, maintenance, and overthrowing of the constitutions of states.[54] Sensing a growing tendency among Americans, including Catholics, to admire the liberal revolutions of the mid-1850's in Europe, Brownson warned of the extreme liberal position which sought political freedom based not on Christian but upon atheistic principles. "The overthrow of our republican constitution would be our political death."[55] Law must remain supreme and continue to protect the rights of minorities. Censoring the radical liberals for their attempts to destroy law and religion, he wrote: "When I hear a man declaiming lustily for liberty, I suspect it is for liberty to pick my pocket, or cut my throat."[56]

When Louis Kossuth, the Hungarian liberal revolutionary came to this country in December, 1851, and received the praise of the press and of the nation's political leaders, Brownson objected to welcoming as a guest of the American nation one who advocated conspiracy "against all legitimate authority, against all religion except an idolatrous worship of what is blasphemously called the *God-People* or the *People-God,* against all morality, all law, all order, and indeed against society itself."[57] When Brownson spoke publicly against Kossuth, his denunciations were greeted with both hisses and applause by his audiences.[58]

Efforts to change the Constitution of Massachusetts in 1853 by having a simple majority suffice to make changes in it led Brownson into the arena of local politics. He again reiterated one of his strongest political convictions: the purpose of a constitution is not merely to confer the power to govern on the majority but to limit its power and thereby to protect the rights of minorities and individuals. Constitutional government checks the absolute power of any group, including the majority and keeps it from placing minorities at the mercy of their arbitrary, and often irresponsible, will.[59] Opponents of the change in the Massachusetts Constitution saw in Brownson an effective instrument to employ in their campaign, and requested his services as a speaker throughout the state. His son, Henry, attributes the defeat of the constitutional revisionists more to his father's efforts than to those of any other one person.[60]

III *The Temporal and Spiritual*

The liberal European revolutions of the mid-nineteenth century still gave Brownson much concern. Too many Americans, including Catholics, were extending their sympathies for the success of these revolutions, and these Americans failed, he thought, to realize that, although fighting under the banner of republicanism, the leaders were infidels seeking to destroy the influence of the Church and the papacy as part of the conservative remnants of European politics. He sought to warn of the rising tide of political atheism—now "wearing a popular or democratic form, as it has since worn an imperial or monarchical form"—because it divorced the state from morality and religion.[61] The desire to have religion play a more prominent role in a nation's political life also necessitated Brownson to write on the proper relationship between the temporal and spiritual powers. But his attempt to delineate the supremacy of the spiritual led to attacks from many Catholics, including members of the hierarchy.

In five successive issues of his *Quarterly Review* in 1853 he offered his views on the powers and relations of the temporal and the spiritual. Both powers received their authority from God, for God is the universal Lord, the sovereign King. The sovereign in all things and over all, God has made his law as universal as his dominion and providence. To Christ, God gave all power in heaven and on earth; and, as God Incarnate, He rules with all power and law. Christ, furthermore, established the Roman Catholic Church as the depository, the guardian, and the judge of his law; and to its apostles and their successors has been given the divine authority to teach this sovereign law to all nations and also to teach them to observe its commandments. Brownson insists, "The commission is to the church, not to the state, and nowhere can it be found that our Lord has made princes, as such, guardians and judges of his law, even in the temporal order."[62]

Christian political philosophers had often declared the supremacy of the Church in spiritual matters, but they extended supremacy in temporal matters to the states, with the Church having a voice in temporal matters that in some way affects man's spiritual concerns and the rights of the Church. Brownson, however, gave the Church a supremacy in all matters and explained this supremacy by proclaiming it as not in itself "precisely temporal" but a "spiritual power, held by a spiritual person, and exerted for a spiritual end."[63] He further explains:

> The temporal order . . . is subjected to the spiritual, and consequently every question that does or can arise in the temporal order is indirectly a spiritual question, and within the jurisdiction of the church as the spiritual authority, and therefore of the pope, who, as supreme chief of the church, possesses that authority in its plenitude. The pope, then, even by virtue of his spiritual authority, has the power to judge all temporal ques-

tions, if not precisely as temporal, yet as spiritual,—for all temporal questions are to be decided by their relation to the spiritual,—and therefore has the right to pronounce sentence of deposition against any sovereign when required by the good of the spiritual order.[64]

Brownson was convinced that he did not enunciate any new theory of Church and state. Pope Gregory VII in the eleventh century considered it his duty to judge the activities of the secular power, refusing the emperor's crown to Prince Henry IV of Germany because of his practice of lay investiture. What Brownson forgot, however, is that this notion of Gregory VII was a theory and not a dogma of the Church, that it was expressed at the height of the feudal Middle Ages to a united Christendom and not to a pluralistic society such as existed in the United States, and that this was the crown of the Holy Roman Empire—a purely papal creation, and not a nation-state.

As for the controversies that have taken place in history between Church and state, the basic question that should have been and would always be asked, according to Brownson, is which of the institutions is supreme. He believes it to be "the traditionary wisdom of mankind" to declare that the spiritual order is supreme and prescribes the law for the temporal."[65] Protestantism receives his condemnation for compromising between the two orders, a compromise that eventually resulted in the total sacrifice of the spiritual and the total supremacy of the temporal.[66]

Brownson's position prohibits man from seeking the spiritual for the sake of the temporal. For, as superior to the temporal, the spiritual determines the end that the temporal is to seek and the means to do so. Regarding the sole end of man as spiritual, man has no temporal end and, therefore, no absolute temporal good. Temporal goods are of value only if they aid man to gain his spiritual ends and are not to be sought as ends in themselves. Such reasoning strengthens Brownson's conviction of the supremacy of the spiritual order exemplified by the Church and the obvious subordinate role of the state to the Church.[67]

What of obedience to temporal authority? Brownson claims that subjects owe allegiance to their legitimate civil rulers. To refuse to obey them or to resist their authority are matters of serious sin against God; for, according to the divine origin of power, there is no authority unless from God and civil rulers rule by divine authority in temporal matters. But as the temporal is subordinate to the spiritual, the spiritual power determines the legitimate rulers and renders judgment on matters of obedience to civil authority.[68]

Having reached a point of obsession with his views on the supremacy of the spiritual over the temporal, Brownson went on to attribute to the Pope the power of deposing secular princes. "The church . . . in deposing a sovereign and absolving his subjects, does not abrogate the law of nature, but simply administers it. She really only declares the law, or pronounces judgment under it."[69] Brownson did not claim that the deposing power of the Pope could be applied to the United States. As a matter of fact, he would reject its use in any modern state since such a doctrine could be applied only if a state were thoroughly Catholic. But in theory, as deduction from the supremacy of the spiritual, he maintained that the Pope could make a juridical declaration stating that a secular prince had forfeited his rights to rule by acts of tyranny.

The bold assertions made by Brownson on the spiritual and temporal orders aroused much indignation on the part of both Catholics and non-Catholics. The criticisms ranged from "importune" to "un-American." The Know Nothings found in his stand one of their strongest arguments against the foreign Catholics: allegiance and obedience to the Pope in Rome preceded their loyalty to the United States. The Nativists could rightly ask, "How can a Catholic be a good American?" The pen of America's most forceful Catholic writer of the time provided fuel for the raging fire of bigotry.

Catholics were no less indignant in their criticism of Brownson's views. Bishop Michael O'Connor of Pittsburgh publicly denounced him for lack of theological soundness. Brownson sought to justify the right to maintain his views and objected to Bishop O'Connor's manner of discrediting him. He wrote to him: "You can bring popular and national prejudice to bear against me. . . . In your article you do not give me fair play before your readers. . . . The doctrine I have defended, if not precisely of faith, is one which I am at liberty to hold, and can hold without reproach."[70] Brownson further stated that his own religious superior, Bishop Fitzpatrick of Boston, had approved his views as a logical deduction of the church's teaching on papal infallibility.[71]

Bishop O'Connor, however, continued his denunciation and publicly replied: "We do not see the necessity of throwing the whole odium which attaches to this or any other article, on his bishop, who, we think, never meant to assume any greater responsibility than what might arise from the assurance that the Review contained nothing contrary to faith or morals."[72] Bishop O'Connor further requested that his name be withdrawn from a letter of the American bishops which indicated approbation of the *Review* and which Brownson had printed on the cover.[73] Archbishop Purcell of Cincinnati censured Brownson's articles as "vagaries" and even predicted that before long he would fall into heresy. Even excommunication was suggested if Brownson did not retract his erroneous views.[74]

Other controversial issues added to the disfavor of Brownson with the hierarchy. His views on Nativism were not received with pleasure, as the hierarchy interpreted them as primarily anti-Irish. Nor did his remarks on Catholic parochial schools lend convincing proof that the converted Catholic wholly supported the stand of the American bishops.[75] Brownson sought to allay the fears of his co-religionists by stating that he entertained orthodox views and had the interest of Catholicism at heart. He wrote letters to the Catholic newspapers that attacked him and offered clarification of his views and a willingness to submit to higher ecclesiastical authority without, of course, sacrificing a determined devotion to principle and to the truth as his conscience saw it.[76]

Efforts to arouse an understanding for his stand on these subjects, however, failed. His own ecclesiastical superior, Bishop Fitzpatrick, did not indicate any needed support; and, during the bishop's absence in Europe, Brownson even published articles without submitting them to the substitute censor. Archbishop Francis P. Kenrick of Baltimore, who once wanted to be regarded as his "sincere admirer and friend," delivered the crushing blow. He requested that Brownson no longer carry the endorsement of the American hierarchy in his magazine because his articles professed "principles at variance with our civil duties." The bishops were thus to be relieved of any sympathy toward views not defined by the church.[77]

When Bishop Fitzpatrick neither publicly nor privately assuaged the enmity of his fellow bishops in regard to Brownson, Brownson decided to leave Boston and to publish the *Quarterly* in New York, a more sympathetic environment. Brownson wrote to a friend in New York, Isaac Hecker, concerning the advisability of a change: "I think I should be with you more in the midst of friends, and I could exert far more personal influence than here. . . . This diocese is becoming more and more Irish. I think I could now get along with his Grace the Archbishop without any serious difficulty, and I think I could breast the storm still raging and likely to rage for some time against me better in New York under his patronage than here."[78] Hecker quickly replied: "This afternoon I called on the Archbishop. In the course of our conversation he mentioned that he had heard that it was your desire to come to New York. I told him it was, with his approbation. He replied that 'he would be quite pleased at your coming, and that if I wrote to you I should tell you so.' These were his words."[79] With this assurance Brownson and his family went to New York in the hope of finding in Archbishop Hughes a more sympathetic and ardent supporter.

Although Brownson answered his harsh critics congenially and without rancor in letters to the Catholic newspapers and to the bishops, he could not help feeling the lack of understanding for his noble intentions. This led to his writing *The Spirit-Rapper,* a work already analyzed and discussed—a more polite counterattack upon those who he thought should have been more receptive to his views.

But Brownson's hope for a more sympathetic environment in New York did not materialize. Archbishop Hughes could not accept Brownson's nationalist sentiments and his views on the relationship between the temporal and the spiritual powers. After two stormy years in New York he decided to take up residence in Elizabeth, New Jersey, and there he continued to express his views.[80]

Noting that one of the more popular objections to the Catholic Church in the United States was its hostility to the American form of government, Brownson wrote an article in the *Quarterly Review* of July, 1856, entitled, "The Church and the Republic."[81]

He contended that the Church is necessary to the republic and that the republic is compatible with the Church. In his analysis of American political and social life, he found two powerful and dangerous tendencies: on the one hand, excessive stress on the power of the state leading to social despotism; on the other hand, an excessive individualism leading to anarchy. Both state and individual were necessary constituents of a constitutional republic, and religion served the purpose of maintaining the balance between these elements as a force independent of them. Because it was higher than both, religion protected the individual against any possible tyranny of the state and restrained the individual from invading the rights of duly constituted authority. But for religion to possess this balancing power it must be organized; for religion without an organization, without a church, was not a power but only an idea or simply opinion and, therefore, an expression of individualism. Brownson could not see in Protestantism the fulfilling of the required balancing role of religion. Either Protestantism was too individualistic—without adequate religious authority defining its dogma, as it encouraged the individual to believe according to his own judgment and interpretation of the Scriptures—or it was too political by depending on the state for its ability to exert any influence on the subjects of a nation, as, for Brownson, was the case in England and in Prussia.

It was to the Catholic Church alone that Brownson felt that America could look for the power of religion to keep the country in balance between the extremes of individualism and state absolutism. For the Catholic Church derived her power not from any government, peoples, or individuals, but from a source above them—God. Her doctrine and discipline were the same for all peoples, whatever their political allegiance; hence, the Church was superior to the state. As for the individual, he was subservient to the Church as the Church is God's divinely instituted authority; he obeyed the state because such obedience, duly and morally exercised, is obedience to God. How did American Catholics fit into the framework of this position? Brownson answered that all that Catholics expected of their government was recognition of the right of conscience to worship God. As this right of conscience lies in the spiritual order in which the state was incompetent, all spiritual questions were to be solved by the private conscience of the citizen and the church. The Catholic Church asked of the American government only its freedom and independence for carrying out its divine mission, and protection only in case of physical attack, since the church employs only a moral and not a physical force to defend her. As for Catholics serving their country, Brownson wrote: "We have in our religion, if we will understand it, and be loyal to its spirit, the conservative power to save the free institutions founded by the patriotism and blood of our heroic fathers. . . . We must cherish an enlightened and generous American patriotism, and labor to consecrate this vast land and its millions of immortal souls to the love of God and our neighbor."[82]

Protestants did not leave unanswered Brownson's views on the inability of their religion to aid effectively the American republic. The *Universalist Quarterly and General Review* of October, 1856, questioned a fundamental point in his argumentation: did religion get its efficacy from organization, or did organization get its efficiency from religion? The fountain of force was religious truth, and an organization was powerless unless held together by the adhesive force of the idea that led individuals to become members of the organization. To this objection Brownson replied that "we derive neither the efficacy of Christianity from organization, nor the efficacy of the organization from Christianity, simply because we do not distinguish them, and hold that Christianity and the church are identically one and the same thing. Christianity is efficacious as the church, because it is only as the church that it exists, or that there is any Christianity."[83]

The *Universalist Quarterly* objected to Brownson's claiming that Christianity and the Roman Catholic Church were identical.[84] Protestants were Protestants simply because they rejected the authority of the Church and preferred to believe that God spoke through the conscience of the individual person. Obviously, Brownson and the Universalists became involved in a theological dispute on the nature of Christianity and the role of any Christian church in effectively spreading the Christian Gospel. In vindication of their respective theological positions, they no longer discussed the issue of the patriotism of Roman Catholics in the American republic. Again, Brownson had apparently convinced neither his co-religionists nor Protestants.

Brownson continued to write articles on the supremacy of the spiritual over the temporal, for the events in European politics further convinced him that many countries were on the road to political absolutism, disregarding the power of the spiritual. Especially did he fear this rise of despotism because of Louis Napoleon's successful *coup d'état* in 1851. He felt that too many were willing to compromise on this important matter: "All attempts, whether by ministers of religion or by ministers of state, to reestablish social peace on the basis of political absolutism, can end only in grave injury both to religion and society. The passion for change has become too strong to be resisted."[85] To those who cried for religious liberty in Europe, Brownson warned that this only meant the usurpation of the spiritual authority by the chief of the state—as had already taken place in England, Prussia, Sweden, Denmark, Norway, Russia, and Turkey.[86]

The adamant Brownson would not yield even to members of the hierarchy because of his firm convictions on the supremacy of the spiritual. Clergymen had their role in the church, but so did laymen, he claimed. He would deny the view which considered that "laymen, in matters of religion, can neither know nor say any thing, that they are . . . interlopers or nullities."[87] He proceeded to distinguish: "We know no law of the church which exempts us as laymen, from our obligation to labor for the promotion of the interests of religion; that imposes on the clergy alone the duty of loving our neighbor and seeking his salvation; or by which we can discharge our moral and religious duties vicariously."[88] Members of the clergy may have to submit to ecclesiastical authority for approval in stating their views, as obedience is one of their vows. But he continued, "The Catholic lay society is not a monastery, and cannot be governed on the monastic principle of obedience."[89]

With such a justification for the expression of his views independently of, and even contrary to, those of the hierarchy, Brownson reiterated his stand on the supremacy of the spiritual over the temporal and went further in his clarification. The supremacy of the Church he defined as supremacy in spiritual matters, and in temporal matters supremacy only in relation to spiritual ends. The Church by divine right, furthermore, determined what things were spiritual and what things were temporal, thus determining her own rights and powers and those of secular society as well. For those matters which the Church determined to be merely temporal, the secular is independent of the spiritual. Spiritual persons have no authority over such matters and can take no part in them by virtue of their spiritual authority.[90]

In making further deductions from his theory of the relationship between the spiritual and the temporal, Brownson considered the temporal sovereignty of the Pope. He did not consider him a spiritual person as the temporal sovereign of Vatican City, since the Pope did not hold that sovereignty by virtue of his spiritual power but by an acquired right. Brownson did regard this papal sovereignty over Vatican City a "very great convenience"; if abolished, its absence might lead to interference in spiritual affairs. But he did recommend a division between the temporal and the spiritual in the Vatican, with the Church abandoning its secular power and remaining simply "the spiritual kingdom of God on earth." For Brownson admitted that as a Roman Catholic he found it embarrassing to champion democracy against absolutism while in Rome itself the Church sustained absolutism in the immediate temporal government through her spiritual head.[91]

Such obstinacy in his views on the temporal and the spiritual —as well as his previous entanglements with the hierarchy on the questions of slavery, Nativism, and parochial schools— brought the attacks on Brownson to a culmination. Bishop Luers of Fort Wayne, Indiana, wrote to him as follows:

> You seem to carry even delicate questions to their *extreme logical consequences* without paying attention to their *practical bearings or results.* . . . For the last six months or more, I have spoken with several bishops, priests, and others, *your real friends and well-wishers,* and they all desire and are extremely anxious to see you drop, for the present, all those irritating questions which have been the source of so much calumny and personal abuse against you.[92]

The importunity of Brownson's views was pointed out by Bishop Elder of Natchez, Mississippi: "You do it in a spirit of grumbling, of general censure of the most odious kind on the Catholic clergy—of holding us all up as willfully guilty of the obnoxious charge made against us by the most bigoted Protestants."[93] Bishop Wood of Philadelphia in 1862 announced that Brownson's *Quarterly Review* ought no longer to be regarded as a Catholic periodical "or [as] a reliable exponent of Catholic doctrines and principles."[94]

Since Brownson refused to submit to the wishes of the American bishops for a halt and even a recantation of his obnoxious views, the expected action took place. Brownson was denounced to Cardinal Barnabò, Prefect of the Congregation of the Propaganda of the Faith in Rome. Brownson attributed the denunciation to Archbishop Purcell, but his son Henry leaned toward Archbishop Hughes as the denunciator, since Hughes had been the object of many of his father's attacks in the matter of disputed questions, and most recently in the controversial article, "The Rights of the Temporal."[95] Fortunately for Brownson, Cardinal Barnabò wrote him personally for a detailed explanation of the charges brought against him. Although admitting a certain perplexity about Brownson's views on the temporal power, Rome found no heresy in the opinion and dismissed the charges on Brownson's assurance that "If my *Review* 'has gone astray,' I am anxious that it should at the earliest moment return to the true path, and I assure his eminence that I have no pride of opinion to gratify, and that the Holy See will always find me a docile and obedient subject."[96]

The failure of Brownson's enemies to secure condemnation only served to intensify his independence: "Heretofore on theological questions our articles have, for the most part, been submitted to theological revision and censorship before publication, hereafter they will not be so submitted. . . . Each number as it appears will be sent to Rome, and any corrections of any sort the Holy See may require or suggest will be most cheerfully made."[97] And he added with a note of triumph: "We hope this explanation will prove satisfactory to all who are willing to be satisfied, and convince those who secretly try to get condemned at Rome a man who is wearing his life out in the cause they profess to have at heart, that Rome only acts with deliberation, and with a sense of justice."[98]

But Rome was not among the paying subscribers to his *Quarterly*, and with the loss of prestige in the United States, brought on by the attacks of the hierarchy, Brownson discontinued publication in October, 1864. It was to his advantage to have ceased publication because in December, 1864, Pope Pius IX issued his famous encyclical, *Quanta Cura,* and the document, *Syllabus of Errors,* both of which condemned all efforts of compromise between the Church and the liberal spirit of the age. Had the *Review* still been published, Brownson's enemies would surely have claimed that it now fell under papal condemnation. As it was, an undercurrent of opinion still placed him in the category of condemnation; but Brownson, writing for the *Ave Maria* magazine, had the opportunity to disclaim condemnation: "Some honest people have supposed that I am myself among those who have incurred the censures of the encyclical, and I have wished to show them that in my own opinion I am not."[99] He went on to demonstrate his innocence: "I hold that the Pope has received from God plenary authority, as the successor of Saint Peter, to teach and to rule the church as supreme pastor and governor, and that whatever he condemns as contrary to the faith I condemn, and whatever he forbids me to do, I cannot do without disobeying God."[100] In 1873 he even claimed that the *Syllabus* and the decrees of the First Vatican Council in 1870 on papal infallibity had justified his position when "it was hardly safe for a poor layman like ourselves to assert the supremacy of the spiritual order, and the subordination of the temporal to the eternal, unless in some vague and indeterminate sense."[101]

IV The American Republic

Brownson's passion for the victory of the Union in the Civil War led to a revision of his political thought. Before embodying the thinking of many years in *The American Republic,* he began in a number of articles the formulation of a philosophical exposition of the American form of government as envisioned by its founders and as modified in the crucible of a century of experience.

The Civil War was a struggle for the life of a nation. This was the basic view that Brownson had regardless of previous sympathy with the Southern way of life. "We support it [the Civil War], and make all the sacrifices in our power to sustain it, as a war for national existence, against a rebellion that seeks to dismember the Union, and destroy our national life."[102] No longer did he expound the States' rights theory; rather he condemned it, especially when it was used to justify the secession of the Southern states from the Union. The basic question resolved itself into which was sovereign, the state or the nation: "whether we are or are not a sovereign nation, with the right of protecting itself against dismemberment or death."[103]

Having rebelled, the seceded states had committed suicide; and, upon their unconditional surrender, the federal government had to permit the people to reorganize themselves into new states.[104] Where was the legal basis for discarding States' rights? For Brownson it existed in the unwritten constitution, antecedent to the written constitution drawn up by the Convention of 1787. This unwritten constitution was "the preexisting constitution of the people themselves, by which they were constituted one political people of the United States."[105] The American republic was founded on the principle of popular sovereignty. The people and not the states established the written Constitution, as is clearly stated in the preamble, "We, the people of the United States . . . do ordain and establish." Furthermore, the people established their own state constitutions as subordinate to the federal constitution and never as contradictory to it, "the supreme law of the land." The states never had acted as separate sovereign states. American independence, and the war to attain it, had been achieved by one joint act made by the colonies united and not the colonies severally.[106] Brownson acknowledged that his views stemmed from John C. Hurd's *The Law of Freedom and Bondage in the United States*, the first volume of which was published in 1858, and the second volume, four years later. The arguments for a strong national government were founded on law and history.[107]

Such was the political and constitutional framework that Brownson used in suggesting methods for dealing with the seceded states during and after the Civil War. He himself had undergone a fundamental change in political philosophy; from a firm believer in States' rights, he became an advocate of a strong federal government.

With the October, 1864, issue Brownson ceased publishing the *Quarterly Review*. Freed from the necessity of meeting journal deadlines and the preoccupation with sundry controversial subjects, provided by his retirement, Brownson now had an op-

portunity he had hardly ever had in his busy journalistic career.
Time for more serious and profound reflection was available,
and he employed this newly found leisure in the writing of *The
American Republic.*

Dedicated to George Bancroft "as a sort of public atonement"
for the harsh criticism made on earlier historical writings, *The
American Republic* is an exposition of Brownson's political
thought. Although the topics of the nature, necessity, extent,
authority, origin, ground, and constitution of government, and
the unity, nationality, constitution, tendencies, and destiny of
the American republic had been discussed in previous writings,
the work is the author's most complete and systematic, as well
as his latest thinking in political thought.[108]

Brownson considered it a necessity for a young nation to examine and realize its mission and destiny. Having adopted a
constitution with no prototype in any prior constitution, he called
for a profound study of its principles to demonstrate its contribution to political science. He pointed out that, while it retained the advantages of constitutions already adopted, it was
unlike any of them and secured advantages which none of these
did, or could, possess. Of particular importance was such a study
in the light of the successful maintenance of the American system after the secession of the Southern states and the Civil War.

Although Brownson claimed that he did not take "bodily"
from any of his previous essays on government, he reiterated
many of his former views. He reasserted the divine origin of
government, with rulers holding their political authority from
God through the people or nation, and the people or nation
holding authority from God through the natural law to designate
their rulers. The people, moreover, had the right to set up their
own constitution; and they also enjoyed the incontestable right
to change their form of government, its magistrates, or its
representatives. Granted that majorities determined a form of
government and its constitution, the rights of minorities were
never taken away; for minorities possessed inalienable rights by
virtue of human nature antecedent to any constitutional document. These notions of government Brownson classified as basic
in the American form of government.

The doctrine of state sovereignty, which Brownson held and
defended from 1828 to 1861, was now rejected. Reasoning from

the principles of government that he advocated, he concluded that God, operating through historical facts, constituted the American people as one political or sovereign people, existing and acting in particular communities called states. This one people organized as states met in convention, framed and established the constitution of government, or instituted a general government in the place of the Continental Congress. The same people, moreover, in respective states, met in convention in each state to frame and establish a particular government for each state individually, which—in union with the general government —constituted the complete and supreme government within the states. The general or federal government, in union with all the particular governments, constituted the complete and supreme government of the nation or whole country.[109]

The answer to two basic questions determined whether one accepted or rejected the States' rights theory. Was United States politically one people, nation, state, or republic—or is it comprised of independent sovereign states united in close and intimate alliance, league, or confederation by a mutual pact or agreement? Were the people of the United States who ordained and established the written constitution one people, or were they not? Reaffirming that the people of the United States acted as one when adopting a federal constitution and that they adopted respective state constitutions as subordinate to the Federal Constitution, Brownson became a firm believer in a strong national government. He did not deny the states their own rights, since he upheld the Tenth Amendment's assurance of States' rights; but he forcefully declared the common good of any one state as subordinate to the common good of the nation.

The profundity and brilliance of Brownson's thinking reached its height in his analysis of the political and religious destiny of America. The special mission of the United States was to continue and complete the Greco-Roman civilization in the political order. On this point, he demonstrated that he was no disdainer of the past but that he wished America to retain all the good in the past as a steppingstone to progress in the future. Although he recognized republican elements in Roman government, he pointed out the great error of the Romans: denial or ignorance of the unity of the human race, as well as of the unity of God. Their sustaining a privileged class and their regarding power as an attribute of birth and of private wealth set limits upon genuine equality of all men.[110] The French and the English improved on the Roman concept of equality, but the former tended to socialism and the latter to pure individualism. The United States had more happily blended the division of powers with recognition of the rights of individuals; moreover, the power of the government on both national and state levels protected these rights and subordinated them to the common good of the people of the whole nation. The continuance of progress in the American democratic system of the balance of equal individual rights and of the powers of government was America's special political mission to the world, for "no greater problem in statesmanship remains to be solved, and no greater contribution to civilization to be made."[111]

Brownson's view of the role of the United States in world politics had the power of prophecy. To the United States would belong the hegemony of the Old World, and "she will have a potent voice in adjusting the balance of power even in Europe."[112] To accomplish this role, the United States needed a great military and naval power. Military preparedness, he insisted, could serve as deterrent to war.

As for the religious destiny of the United States, Brownson sought not "to create a new religion nor to found a new church."[113] He would have religion stand above and independent of the state, with neither the state absorbing the Church nor the Church absorbing the state. Both Church and state were to move freely according to their own natures and proper spheres. Although externally they might be governing bodies, both Church and state were united in the interior principles which granted them vitality and force so that each could fulfill its respective mission. "The effect of this mission of our country fully realized, would be to harmonize Church and state, religion and politics, not by absorbing either in the other, or by obliterating the natural distinction between them, but by conforming both to the real or divine order, which is supreme and immutable."[114] Brownson gave full recognition to the fact that the United States was a pluralistic society, that "false religions are legally as free as the true religion."[115] An established or preferred religion would have no place in American democratic society; furthermore, having one would contradict the very nature of the independence of religion and the state, and would result in making religion a civil institution.[116]

Brownson had high praise for the framework in which the Catholic Church could perform its religious mission in this country. Without any intervention or mediation of the state, the Church enjoyed freedom to act according to her own constitution and laws, and she exercised her own discipline on her own spiritual subjects. "The church being free, and the state harmonizing with her, catholicity has, in the freedom of both, all the protection it needs, all the security it can ask, all the support it can, in the nature of the case, receive from external institutions, or from social and political organizations."[117]

Brownson had now come to reason like most of his fellow Catholics in the United States. He discarded his old views on the supremacy of the spiritual over the temporal—views that had only served to increase the Protestants' questioning of the loyalty of American Roman Catholics and to undermine his influence with co-religionists and members of the Catholic hierarchy. Had Brownson been less belligerent and adamant in his previous views regarding the relation of Church and state in this country, *The American Republic* would have had a much wider audience. As it was, and apparently still is today, Brownson's fear of his book's being "neglected" was justified."[118] If readers, however, could have forgotten Brownson's previous rashness, they would have found in *The American Republic* a political testament of profound thought on both the political and religious mission of American Catholics, and a contribution to a better understanding of America's great experiment in political thinking.[119]

Maynard considers *The American Republic* the "best" of Brownson's works.[120] Donovan has even gone so far as to label it the greatest book on general politics written by an American.[121] Schlesinger has classified the book as "closely reasoned and, in a strange way, full of keen insights into American government," but he has also added that, by the time it was written, Brownson had "ruined all chances of getting an unbiased hearing."[122] George Ripley, a friend of long-standing, predicted the reception of the book by readers who would "admire his skill in combination and his fertility of resource with the same wonder with which they watch the movements of an adroit chess player."[123]

One of Brownson's last writings, "The Democratic Republic," in the April, 1873, issue of the *Quarterly Review*, is another well-thought-out exposition of his political views. After a brief résumé of previous stands on democracy, he reiterated his faith in democracy as the "supremacy of man over his accidents," which, when defined, means that democracy regards "the man as more than his possessions, social position, or any thing separable from his manhood."[124] Only with such a view of democracy could the Declaration of Independence have contained the great democratic principle that "governments derive their just powers from the consent of the governed." And such a view recognized that the will of the people was the most direct and authentic expression of the divine will that could be had or desired. "The American Constitution is not founded on political atheism, but recognizes the rights of man and, therefore, the rights of God."[125]

Because Brownson saw in the American Constitution a divine ordination of political authority, he urged Americans as citizens and as government officials to live according to the highest ideals of the Christian tradition. If Americans perverted their freedom and interpreted it as emancipation from moral restraints, democracy then paved the way for avarice, dishonesty, fraud, corruption. Rather, he insisted, American politics must never sever itself from the moral order.

A study of Brownson's political thought from the writing of *The American Republic* demonstrates how—as Cook and Leavelle have analyzed it—he struck the balance between "a moderate conservatism and a constructive liberalism."[126] Brownson graduated from the youthful radicalism that was unrelated to social and moral realities and yet avoided a static conservatism that would resist change in a constantly changing society. Brownson thus showed that true liberalism and true conservatism need not be necessarily opposed on basic approaches to solutions of problems; actually they are two sides of the same coin. Such a balance gives Brownson's political thought "its significance and appositiveness today."[127]

CHAPTER 4

The Literary Critic

ORESTES BROWNSON has been treated as a searcher for religious truth, as a social reformer, and as a political philosopher; but it was largely through the medium of literary criticism that he wrote in these areas of thought. In a period of over forty years as an editor and journalist, he reviewed well over five hundred books of American and European authors, with subjects ranging over many areas of thought. The analyses and criticisms in these books often occasioned the formulation of his own views. Although he was by profession a journalist, his penetration into the inner life of society with the formulation of philosophical principles to guide it has transcended the dimensions of journalism. Whether or not one can agree with Brownson, it must be acknowledged that his comments and analyses are valuable for a study of the religious, socio-economic, and political thought of the nineteenth century and that they served to stimulate thinking on the great issues of his day.

In seeking to evaluate various writers, Brownson admitted the difficulty arising from a lack of some recognized standard by which to judge literary works. Without a science or philosophy of art, all literary criticism is unscientific, empirical, founded on habit, prejudice, or changing fashion. Since art seeks to realize the beautiful, basic to an objective appreciation of art would be an adequate ontology. The true ontology for Brownson is expressed in the first verse of the Book of Genesis: "In the beginning God created heaven and earth." Art may be defined as the "imitation . . . of the divine activity as first cause, or creator, and is, therefore, in the order of second causes, creative."[1] True beauty is the splendor of the Creator; but such a notion of beauty requires a religious faith. Only a profoundly religious age can produce or appreciate the sublime forms of art. He therefore asks artists to be less psychological and more philosophical.

By requiring adherence to the standards of religious belief in literary and artistic endeavors, Brownson does not ask the poet and writer to become a philosopher or theologian, to make sermons out of literary productions. Their task is to aim

> at the expression of the beautiful; but the beautiful is the form of the true, and cannot be found where the true is wanting. We are not so unreasonable as to ask of the poet a system of metaphysics or a code of ethics; we do not ask the artist to leave his own proper department, and to enter that of science; we understand the distinct sphere of art, and highly appreciate it,—more highly perhaps, than we get credit for; but we do contend that no man can be a true poet, or artist, who has in his mind a false speculative system. His mind must be informed with ideal truth, or he can never apprehend or express true beauty of form; and all ideal truth pertains to the department of speculative science. The poet must know as well as feel, and know principles, the eternal verities of things, in their normal order and relations, or his expression will be broken, confused, the ebullition of lawless passion, the extravagances of a wild and inconstant fancy, or the incoherent ravings of folly and madness.[2]

For Brownson, then, religion forms the standard of literary criticism. In doctrinal matters, the standard is furnished by his Catholic faith and morals; in matters of style, by a philosophy of art based on a Christian interpretation of the nature of the world as being the handiwork of God's creation.[3] But, in this latter aspect of art, the Roman Catholic Church leaves much room for discussion; and the history of Christian art and literature is replete with different styles. In all his literary reviews Brownson adopts as his standard of criticism the subjects, doctrines, principles, or tendencies of the books, rather than the books themselves as mere literary productions. "We prize literature only as they subserve Christian doctrine and morals."[4]

Literature for literature's sake was not the delight of Brownson. Content, not form; ideas, not language, were his literary criteria.[5] Rightfully, therefore, can Schlesinger point out Brownson's limitations as a literary critic: "He considered works of art out of the corner of his eye and always in the light of more burning questions."[6]

I *American Literature*

In 1843 Brownson set forth a criterion for a literature truly characteristic of America. He desired a literature that "breathes a free, noble, and generous spirit; that is full of the love of man as man; and kindles up a holy ardor in all who come under its influence, and imparts to them the needed wisdom, to labor for the moral, the religious, the intellectual, and the physical well-being of all men, especially of the poorer, and more numerous classes."[7]

It was not to be a literature accommodated to the bents and apprehension of the majority of the people. Leveling itself to the masses would only give a superficial and feeble view of American life. Literature for democracy would not be his slogan; for that implies the bringing of thought to the level of "the narrow views, crude notions, and blind instincts of the multitude."[8] Literature's duty is not in reflecting but in instructing and elevating the masses; but he found the United States lacking in such a literature: "American literature can scarcely be said to have a being."[9] Brownson wanted to see an array of books portraying American free institutions, appealing to the higher faculties of the soul, and being considered the embodiment of our national life.

The reasons for a lack of such literature in this country Brownson attributes to want of faith in the intellect and to lack of confidence in ourselves. Preoccupation of the whole nation in the pursuit of wealth, in the development of the material resources of a potentially rich nation, has so absorbed us that attention to intellectual endeavors has been lacking. Having progressed in economic matters, it is now time to create a literature deserving of the world's admiration.

Nor was Brownson alone in urging a literature truly characteristic of this country. William Ellery Channing had made a similar appeal because he believed literature to be "among the most powerful methods of exalting the character of a nation, of forming a better race of men."[10] Yet Brownson emphasized that deliberate attempts to produce a national literature are somewhat ridiculous: a genuine national literature is a spontaneous expression of the life of a nation. Only writers impassioned with the ideals of American free institutions could truly embody in their writings the aspirations of the nation they love.

As for the meagerness of American literature Brownson felt that the long dependency of the colonies on England was responsible. Colonists were in the habit of looking to England for direction in all areas and of considering the mother country as their intellectual and moral superior. This feeling can be partially justified since England had occupied a position of preeminence in political, economic, and literary endeavors. Whatever efforts Americans made, especially in literature, amounted to nothing more than "servile imitation" in childlike devotion to the mother country. "In seeking to write as Englishmen, [we] abdicated our power to write as Americans."[11] To the objection that originality cannot readily be had, he concedes that many things have been said, but he also asserts that originality consists in expressing, in one's own distinctive way, what one has personally thought, felt, or lived. No two individuals share exactly the same experiences in life; our experiences, therefore, have a distinctive character and the expression of these experiences is the claim to authorship. The literary artist achieves recognition for expressing "what is truest, deepest, richest, and broadest in his own human nature."[12] Even the great Shakespeare reiterated many things already said, but he put his own personality in the writings that have given him renown.

In reviewing some years later Bayard Taylor's *Hannah Thurston; a Story of American Life,* published in 1864, Brownson praises the author's efforts to produce a work depicting American life. He admits that the book shows some experience of life, true powers of observation, some humor and unobtrusive wit. But the author, he claims, strikes one not as a man of deep feeling or of original and far-reaching thought: "He designs well, constructs not unhappily the outlines of his story, gives us its dry bones properly arranged, and proves himself a good literary anatomist; but he succeeds not in clothing them with living flesh, nor in breathing a soul into the body, and bidding it live."[13] Why? Simply because Taylor the American plays the Englishman and, therefore, reflects the English nature of more heart than soul. But Taylor ought not to be blamed, as "literature is the exponent of the life and character of the people who produce it. The stream cannot rise higher than its fountain."[14]

Brownson's insistence on a national literature of the highest caliber led to his discouraging those efforts toward the mere production of any kind of literature by American writers. He took issue in 1847 with *The Literary World,* a gazette for authors, readers, and publishers that aimed to lead to a preference for American authors. Seeing this as a venture to make literature an end in itself, Brownson emphasized the notion of literature as a means to "instruct us in that which it is necessary for us to know in order to discharge, or the better to discharge our duties as moral, religious, and social beings."[15] Attempts at wholesale publication of writings by authors solely because they are Americans would not advance the cultural tone of the nation, nor provide a worthy literature. When we consider Brownson's condemnation of efforts commonly regarded as literature, we find his words suitable also for an evaluation of some of the present-day best-sellers:

> Every dapper little fellow, every sentimental young lady, or not young, married unhappily, or despairing of getting married, who can scribble a few lines each beginning with a capital letter, or dash off a murderous tale about love, or an amorous tale about murder, is encouraged to turn author by profession, and finds no lack of opportunity to aid in deluging the land with nonsense, cant, sentimentality, sensuality, obscenity, and blasphemy.[16]

Brownson would not venture a prediction of the future of American literature, but he did notice an increasing depth and earnestness among American writers, who, if adhering to the principles of free thought in America, should produce a literature truly characteristic of our free institutions.

The comments of Brownson on some American authors are interesting, although not in conformity with most generally held evaluations of their works. His main criticism of Ralph Waldo Emerson is directed toward Emerson's false philosophy. A Transcendentalist, Emerson views beauty as something in man himself, dependent solely on his own internal state and his manner of seeing himself and the world around him. Despite Emerson's rich and fervid imagination, refined taste, exquisite sensibility, a strong and acute intellect, and a warm and loving heart, Brownson states that the best he could say of Emerson's poems is that they indicate the longing of his spirit for truth, a morality, a freedom, a peace which he feels—and laments that he does not have.[17]

As a prose writer Emerson is praised by Brownson: "No living writer surpasses him in his mastery of pure and classic English, or equals him in the exquisite delicacy and finish of his chiseled sentences, or the metallic ring of his style."[18] But he finds little sympathy for Emerson's philosophical basis for his Transcendentalist views and for his hesitancy to study the claims of the Roman Catholic Church, the religion in which Brownson feels that Emerson can discover both the transient and the permanent in life.[19]

In James Russell Lowell's *The Vision of Sir Launfal,* published in 1848, Brownson finds a sentimental morality, an ignorance of the basic principles of ethical science. As a poet, Lowell may possess a lively fancy, a quick eye for the beauties of nature, and considerable facility of expression. Lacking a sound philosophy, however, renders Lowell unable to go beyond the evidence of his senses and to express the beauty of moral truth:

> With solid training under the direction of religion and sound philosophy, which would have given elevation to his soul, clearness to his view, firmness to his will, and sanctity to his aims, he would have been a poet. He has no complaint to bring against nature. He has, if we may so speak, genius enough potentially, and artistic genius; but he has neither been subjected to the discipline, nor has he submitted himself to the serious and patient labor of thought, necessary to reduce the potentiality of his nature to act.[20]

In *The Vision of Sir Launfal,* Lowell sought to modernize the external character of the old legend of the knights in search of the Holy Grail, but he also ended up in changing its internal character. The moral of the old legend consisted in the merit of the virtue of chastity as it affected the whole personality of an individual. But Lowell dispensed with this moral as foreign to the ideas and habits of moderns, a moral more likely to offend than to interest the people of modern times. Brownson, therefore, condemns this moral maneuvering of human behavior that acts, not on motives, but on one's feelings.[21]

A review of Henry Ward Beecher's *Norwood; or, Village Life in New England,* published in 1868, occasioned brief remarks on other literary members of the Beecher family, all children of Lyman Beecher, a Presbyterian minister: Doctor Edward, known for books hostile to Roman Catholicism, and Harriet Beecher Stowe, author of *Uncle Tom's Cabin.* "The Beecher genius is not lyrical or dramatic, but essentially militant and prosaic."[22] They lack purity of taste, refined culture, classical grace and polish, creative power. Their success as writers stems from their championing popular causes: "They are of the world, and the world loves them."[23]

In the review of *Norwood,* a description of life in the town of Norwood, Connecticut, Brownson denies the truth of Henry Ward Beecher's observation that the New England Puritans were "a set of gloomy fanatics, austere, unbending, harsh and cruel, minding everybody's business but their own."[24] Beecher, furthermore, generalized the character of all of the New England states from village life in a Connecticut valley town, and he failed to observe the marked differences of character among the people of the several states. Brownson points out that, in the matter of wit, for example, the Massachusetts man is classical and refined; the Connecticut man, sly and not incapable of being coarse; the Vermonter, satirical and humorous. Brownson condemned Beecher's exaggerations of New England Puritanism, and he defended the Puritan influence for keeping alive in the community a certain Christian habit of thought, a belief in the necessity of supernatural grace, and regard for a Christian conscience.[25]

An American with whose writings Brownson had sympathy is Richard H. Dana. In his moral and political essays Dana expressed reservation on rule by the majority of the people; for he viewed such rule as mobocracy rather than as a rule which showed respect for the rights of minorities regardless of majority whims. Brownson even places Dana at the head of American poets, and he praises in particular his quick eye for external beauty, exquisite pictures of nature, natural and easy poetical language, and a style that is clear, strong, terse, and free from all exaggerations and diffuseness. As a prose writer Dana is, says Brownson, unsurpassed among Americans because of his clearness, precision, naturalness, purity, and the classic grace and finish of his style and diction.[26]

Brownson attributes to Daniel Webster all the terseness of Demosthenes, the grace and fullness of Cicero, the fire and energy of Chatham, and a dignity and repose peculiarly his own. Webster inspires one, as listener or reader, with orations which bespeak strength and modesty. He is classified as America's best rhetorician and as worthy of the assiduous study of the young literary aspirant. As a master of style, Webster is free and natural, instructive and pleasing, pure and correct, graceful and elevated, dignified and noble.[27]

George Bancroft is criticized for his historical methodology. Brownson claimed that, rather than let the facts of history speak for themselves, Bancroft began with a theory and then chose only facts which substantiated his theory: "He simply uses history for the purpose of setting forth, illustrating, confirming, and disseminating his speculative theories on God, man, and society."[28] In 1852, although considering Bancroft a brilliant and fascinating writer, Brownson rejected him as a genuine historian.[29] But, as he did with so many issues in later years, Brownson changed his estimate of Bancroft. He dedicated *The American Republic* to him, "the erudite, philosophical, and eloquent historian of the United States . . . as a slight homage to genius, ability, patriotism, private worth, and public service."[30]

James Fenimore Cooper stands high in Brownson's estimation as an author distinguished for the molding of America's literary character. He offers a different evaluation of Cooper's earlier and later works. For affording the reader an amusing tale, the earlier works are superior; but they stand as inferior to his later works in depth of thought, solidity of principles, and high moral aims. He gives preference to his later works as attempts to correct the foibles, errors, and dangerous tendencies of his countrymen, and to the earlier works as they sought to defend American character and institutions against the aspersions and prejudices of Europeans.[31] Commenting on Cooper's *Ways of the Hour*, Brownson applauds the author's call for a complete emancipation of woman from the old pagan doctrine which regarded her as a chattel. Although Brownson granted that the book would have no appeal for the young, the giddy, and the sentimental, he assures pleasure and instruction for the thoughtful, the cultivated and refined, the Christian, and the moralist—

as well as much enjoyment of the scenes and incidents of great beauty and power depicted in the work.[32]

As for Nathaniel Hawthorne, his creative mind is praised, and he is considered the first writer about whom American literature can boast. But Brownson repudiates *The Scarlet Letter* on moral and religious grounds. The main characters of the book never really repent of their crime; their pride is injured but not their consciences. Although he gives praise to the manner in which the story is told—with great naturalness, ease, grace, and delicacy—he affirms that the story should never have been told.[33] In an evaluation of Hawthorne and Washington Irving together, Brownson praises them for their good taste and their unaffected, natural, simple, easy, and graceful style; but he considers them as lacking strength and dignity. "They are pleasant authors for the boudoir, or to read while resting one's self on the sofa after dinner."[34]

Brownson's views on women novelists are rather interesting. Although an advocate of profound reverence for womanhood, he decried the fact that women produce such a large share of popular literature.[35] He objects to women novelists because they tend "to emasculate thought, to enervate the mind, or to foster a weak and watery sentimentalism or a corrupting sensationalism."[36] In referring to the image of womanhood portrayed by women novelists, Brownson notes that a distorted view is presented; they make the female appear as "heartless, capricious, despotic, intriguing, greedy of power, and indifferent to the misery and ruin she may bring upon those she is bound by every tie of nature and religion to love and cherish if they come between her and her purpose."[37]

However, Brownson was not completely one-sided on women as writers. He bestowed praise on George Sand (Madame Dudevant), on Lady Georgiana for her novel *Mrs. Geraldine's Niece*, and on a few Catholic mystical writers, such as St. Theresa and St. Catherine. Brownson did feel that woman's virtue and refinement could serve to inspire and elevate the masculine intellect in literary creations.[38]

Because the majority of the American Catholic population was made up of illiterate laborers, Brownson could not hope for a literary public large enough to give adequate encouragement to Catholic authors. Moreover, he felt that the general feeling of

Protestants toward Catholics did not favor recognition of
Catholic literary endeavors. Yet he was looking forward to an
estimable Catholic-American literature as Catholics improved
their intellectual status through education.[39]

Truly did Brownson think that the time was approaching
when Catholics would make large contributions to an American
national literature. They, too, like all other American writers
must not fall into the danger of merely copying from models of
the Old World national literatures. Our political independence
postulates also a literary independence. Catholics' claim to
originality in literary pursuits stems from the fact that for the
first time in the history of Christendom there exists a civil order
in harmony with the Church's principles. With the exception of
the literature of the Church, the literatures of the Old World
have been exponents of pagan civilizations and not in harmony
with the mind and spirit of the Church. Even popular national
literature of Catholic Europe Brownson considers as only
partially Catholic because European literature is markedly either
sacred or profane. To imitate European literature would lead
Americans to retain and exaggerate this variance between
religion and literature, as well as to ignore a marked difference
in political institutions.[40]

What is to be the purpose of an American Catholic literature?
Brownson quickly discards those writings which are for the
cloister or theological in purpose. In such writings the Church
already abounds, and these can be produced in any age or nation. Rather, Catholics should aim "to cultivate, refine, and
humanize barbarous nature, and to remove those obstacles to
the introduction and progress of Catholic civilization. . . . The
office of popular literature is not precisely to spiritualize, but
to civilize a people."[41] As an example of an area where Catholics could make a contribution Brownson cites modern novels
and romances which make an improper use of the sentiment of
love and marriage. Such authors write from fancy and not from
life; they lead young people to expect from marriage a paradise
never realizable on earth. Catholic writings on love and marriage, although not theological treatises, could present a thoroughly Christian view and so tend to civilize.

The civilizing aim of Catholic literature could also be used to
affect the indocile and rebellious spirit of modern poetry and

romance. Adherence to an objective moral law should be idealized in contradistinction to modern literature's exaltation of unbridled freedom at the expense of law and order. Although Catholics should write to meet the literary needs and tastes of all, it is the youth who most needs a proper orientation to life. Experience teaches that we have to go beyond the Bible, the prayer book, and the manual of meditations. Unless Catholics furnish a popular literature free from corrupting tendencies but equally attractive to their literary wants and tastes, youth will resort to the corrupting literature of the day. The challenge is to provide what Brownson terms a *Christian secular culture,* the ability "to breathe into literature the true Catholic spirit."[42] Thus could the secular element of individual and social life be brought into the service of religion in the same manner that the Church makes use of poetry and music in the celebrating of divine worship or of art in the construction and decoration of her altars and houses of worship.

As a former Protestant, Brownson was well aware of American Protestantism's view of the Roman Catholic Church as opposed to liberty of the press and thought. An article in the *Methodist Quarterly Review* gave him an opportunity to present the Roman Catholic Church's contribution to learning.[43] He cites the role of monasticism in the preservation of ancient literature and in the early formation of a Christian literature, even in the so-called "Dark Ages." For every period of history he brings forth leading Christian writers as representative of a Church devoted to encouraging learning. He justifies censorship, as for example *The Index* of forbidden books, for the same reason that a parent supervises the moral and spiritual development of his child. That unlimited freedom of the mind is preached by any religious denomination he denies, for all religions require adherence to a set body of truths and do not consider one in good standing in the practice and worship of one's faith if these requirements are ignored.

While decrying a genuine American literature or "our regular built books," Brownson, in his years as a social radical, saw in American newspapers a claim to American popular literature:

> Our newspapers are conducted for the great mass of the people,
> by men who come out immediately from the bosom of the people,
> and they of necessity express the sentiments of the people. They

constitute, therefore, in the strictest sense of the word, a popular literature. And scattered through our newspapers and popular journals, may be found more fine writing, more true poetry, genuine eloquence, vigorous thought, original and comprehensive views, than can be found in the classics of either France or England. All the elements of the soul by turns are appealed to, and in turn find their expression; all subjects are discussed, and on all sides too; and often with a clearness and depth which leave little to be desired.[44]

Brownson praised the press for stimulating thought and discussion among the people about urgent and timely topics. He even envisioned the newspaper as the means of preparing for an American literature, for the press could create a taste for literature and could thereby increase the demand for more elaborate literary productions.[45]

The above views, however, were expressed before the election of 1840. Loss of faith in the people led also to loss of respect for the role of the press in championing causes in a manner independent of a newspaper's readers and subscribers, because

the press depends on the people, and must conform to their opinions, passions, prejudices, and tendencies, or they will not support it. Besides, the independent press, so called, is the chief corruptor of the people, and we owe to it, and the secular press generally, the low moral tone of the public, the growing religious indifference of the community, the shameless sacrifice of principle to success; truth and justice, wisdom and virtue, to popularity. We might as well look to Satan to correct sin, as to the press to apply a remedy to the growing evils and destructive tendencies of the American people.[46]

Even as a stimulant to thought did Brownson later reject the value of the press: "Its natural tendency is to bring literature down to the level of the tastes and attainments of the unreasoning, undisciplined, and conceited multitude, and to lessen the demand for patient thought, sound learning, and genuine science."[47]

In asking for an educated class as an indispensable condition for the progress of the people, Brownson sees the press as tending "to make literature light, shallow, and unprofitable" and to make the public mind unfit for a literature of a more respectable character. For "a people accustomed to read only newspapers and the light trash of the day can relish nothing else."[48]

As for the Catholic press, however, Brownson sees it as free from the dependence on the people as the secular press ordinarily is. While the non-Catholic press proceeds from the principle that the people are the jury and that its editors must render verdicts in the people's favor if they are to have readers and subscribers, the Catholic press proceeds from the principle that it has the duty to make known to the people the judgment of the court, which is the Church. The Catholic press is an organ of the Church as God's teaching authority on earth and not the organ of the people.[49] This view is in accord with Brownson's concept of the church as free and independent of all forces and as subject to no one but God in expounding and defending truth.[50]

II   *European Literature*

Possibly more than any American of his time, Brownson was well acquainted with the literature of different European nations. He had read and reviewed European authors for his *Quarterly* and other periodicals.

On the whole, Brownson does not consider as justified the charges of indecency, licentiousness, and a tendency toward anti-socialism that had been made about modern French literature by some American literary critics. Yet from such a refined and highly civilized people he has not received the pleasure and profit that ought to be expected. He refers to Balzac as a writer of "great power and fertility," a master in laying open the vices and corruptions of society. But Balzac leads the reader to contempt for mankind, and he leaves the reader with no strong desire to make society better or more favorable to the growth of virtue and happiness. "We rise from his pages soured, indignant, and misanthropic"[51]

As for Victor Hugo, Brownson disagrees with his theory of art which substitutes the grotesque for the beautiful and the horrible for the pathetic. By no means wanting in genius, talent, and learning, "he gives us works which chill, rather than please, and harrow up nerves, instead of melting the heart."[52] Although he considered Alexandre Dumas inferior to Hugo in talent and genius and not so cold and freezing as Balzac, Dumas at least looks at the brighter side of things and lends himself to warmer sympathies and a more genial spirit.[53]

In the highly censured George Sand, Brownson sees a writer of great ability and powerful genius, more illustrious than any other female writer with whom he is acquainted in ancient or modern literature. Although adept in exposing vice, she is not alone in the usual French spirit of mere wantonness, but she does nourish the hope of aspiring to something better.[54]

There does exist, however, a wholesome characteristic of modern French literature. It is impregnated with social democracy, a recognition of the rights and dignity of the masses. It does not court the aristocracy, for its heroes need not have titles and vice is exposed in high places. The masses are not treated with ridicule and contempt but with compassionate understanding.[55]

Catholics in France are attempting to produce a popular literature of their own, but it is smothered by a general popular literature that is irreligious, immoral, and cynical. As the readers of this literature form an overwhelming majority of the population, French literature could not have its wide circulation without their support. Brownson, therefore, accuses the French of thinking that they can be Catholic in one department of life and atheistic in other departments at the same time.[56]

Out of the political revolutions of modern Germany there arises in its literature "a clear and piercing voice to utter for the poor, the friendless, and the down-trodden."[57] Brownson classifies German Catholic literature as the most solid, erudite, and vigorous in modern times; unfortunately, however, it is not known outside Germany.[58]

As for Italy, her writers bespeak political unsettlement and the delicate position of the Holy See. Although learned and able, the writers "move as men in chains," in an air of timidity and restraint. Brownson partially justifies this condition on the grounds that any publication from Rome would be looked upon as at least a semi-official view of the Catholic Church with the Pope sharing some responsibility for its statements.[59]

Engaged in a life and death struggle to defend their religion and nationality, the Irish have not been in a situation favorable to the free and full development of the Irish spirit and genius. If they would be given a more favorable milieu, however, Brownson predicts a glorious future in producing the richest and purest

Catholic literature the world has known; for they have all the natural genius and qualities required to do so—provided that, in the struggle for freedom, their Catholic faith is not lost. But in the nineteenth century too many Irish writers are torn between loyalty to the nation or to their faith; and it has become difficult to classify their works in the category of popular *Catholic* literature or of popular Irish *national* literature.

English literature, in Brownson's opinion, surpasses that of all modern nations in genuine works of imagination. But, strictly speaking, the English lack a national poetry, national songs, and national airs. This is due to the fact that, as a practical people, they have made industry and commerce their national songs: "They have, after all, a national song in the steam-engine and deep-laden ship, and national music in the ringing of the ever-busy hammer of industry."[60] Preoccupation with material prosperity has led them to pagan gloom, to a literature that is dry and cold, "or the wail of the stricken heart."[61] Brownson undoubtedly alludes to the thought of Carlyle who had written in *Past and Present* a work influential in Brownson's social and economic thinking,[62] "England is full of wealth, of multifarious produce, supply for human want in every kind; yet England is dying of inanition."[63] Brownson labels this judgment "the wail of a truly manly heart, over the misery and wretchedness he sees everywhere around."[64] Carlyle also contrasted in his work English society under feudalism and the Catholic Church with society under Protestantism and the industrial order.

When, however, England was Catholic, Brownson was to conclude, she was known the world over as "Merry England," and she possessed a gladsome and smiling literature. Having withdrawn from Catholicism, England followed the lot of all Protestant nations, whose "epic is one long monotonous plaint of woe, or unearthly howl of despair."[65] Protestant ascetic literature depicts God as hard and austere, cruel and tyrannical; it presents no Father's love and awakens no filial affection. Milton and Byron read like lamentations.[66] As for Milton, he "had a happy knack of interpreting the thought of devils, for he was himself a superb rebel, and a spirit kindred to Satan."[67]

Brownson praises Wordsworth's command of poetical language, the harmony and liquid sweetness of his verses; but he takes issue with his ontology: Wordsworth was too pantheistic, viewing God and the world as indistinguishable. His descriptions of nature, although very true and the result of careful observation, fail to illustrate any truth, teach any lesson—all due to a false theory that the ideal which the artist must seek to realize in forms of his own creation is in the mind itself, and is projected from the soul instead of being apprehended by it.[68]

As to the style of two prominent English philosophers, Brownson seldom finds any difficulty in arriving at the meaning of Locke's and of Hobbes's ideas. Locke's style is diffuse, verbal, tedious, and lacking in elegance, precision, and vigor. Hobbes surpasses Locke in strength, precision, and compactness. Hobbes, moreover, can tell the reader more in a few short sentences than Locke can in an entire long chapter.[69]

Brownson appears to have been more familiar with Thomas Carlyle than with any other English author. He had reviewed his *Past and Present* and *The French Revolution*. And he considered him "a thorough master of language," whose style is "natural, free from all literary primness and affectation, sincere, earnest, forcible,—admirably adapted to all the natural undulations of the soul; and, when read aloud, to those of the voice."[70] Brownson acknowledges Carlyle's effort as a historian "to give the most conscientious desire of seeing things exactly as they are, and describing them with scrupulous truth."[71] But he feels that Carlyle's tendency to hero worship equates history with biography.[72] He furthermore frequently reduces the supernatural to the natural, while apparently attempting to assert the supernatural.[73]

Commended as models for all who aspire to make a contribution to Catholic literature are Cardinal Wiseman's *Essays on Various Subjects*, a three-volume work published in 1853. Brownson found these essays unlike most theological works, so frequently written in dry, formal, and stiff scholastic form. Dealing with scriptural, historical, and Catholic devotional practices, these essays are marked "by great clearness of apprehension and expression, depth and originality of thought, a rich imagination, a cultivated taste, and a tender devotional spirit."[74] Brownson praises Wiseman's evaluation of the role of the Oxford Movement in English ecclesiastical history, especially since Wiseman refuted the errors of the men engaged in this movement in a manner that retained their respect and possibly even their affection.[75]

With John Henry Newman, a convert to the Roman Catholic Church, Brownson engaged in a theological controversy. He branded as heretical Newman's *An Essay on the Development of Christian Doctrine*, which stated that there had been "a real progress of the church in her own apprehension and understanding of the sacred deposit of faith committed to her charge."[76] Brownson, on the other hand, maintained that "the church has no natural history, for she is not in the order of nature, but of grace."[77] Charges and countercharges between the two writers and their supporters appeared in letters and periodicals.[78] Although the two converts could not quite fully agree on this theological point, they did manage to find occasion for mutual praise. Brownson described Newman as clear and acute as a thinker and as choice and exact as a writer. Despite his "purely inductive mind" and the inevitable disadvantages of it in molding his views, "no man has . . . a clearer or keener sight than he, and no man can more clearly, vividly, distinctly, accurately, or forcibly express what he thus apprehends."[79] Brownson, however, fared better at the hands of Newman. Upon appointment as rector of the Catholic University of Dublin, Newman offered to Brownson one of the professorial chairs at the university. Although Brownson did not consider it advisable to accept, Maynard has judged that "it was perhaps the highest honor and handsomest tribute that Brownson ever received."[80]

CHAPTER 5

Lover of Truth

IN 1864, at a time in his life when the anger and distrust of both Catholics and non-Catholics were highest against him, Brownson expressed the motif of his life and work: "From our youth up we have loved truth, and wooed her as a bride, and we wish to die in her embrace."[1] For Brownson, whether searching for a religion to embrace, espousing a social cause, defending a political issue, evaluating a literary work, always did so in the interest of seeking the truth. Many motives can influence journalists and social leaders: financial gain, popularity, a host of readers and followers. But truth can be said to be the *raison d'être* of Brownson's life and writings. Isaac Hecker could well say of him, "His predominant passion was love of truth. This was all his glory and all his trouble; all his quarrels, friendships, aversions, perplexities, triumphs, labors."[2]

By attributing to Brownson so noble a title as lover of truth, it is not implied that he always achieved it or that he was right on all the issues about which he wrote or defended. Nor can the manner in which he frequently battled with opponents be characterized by the humility and forbearance indicative of a lover of truth. Rather his greatness lies not in being right and polite but in possessing an unswerving dedication to principle as he saw it. "Controversy was meat and drink to him; logic, not sweet reasonableness, was his weapon."[3]

One may disagree with the reasons that Brownson offered for shifting from one religious affiliation to another. But he explains each religious change. Restless human hearts can find rest only when they are at peace with their God. Hypocrisy in all matters, and most especially religious matters, is condemned. Devout adherence to a religious faith implies in its very nature an acceptance of its beliefs and practices. God not only loves the cheerful giver but the sincere believer as well. But Brownson, the lover of religious truth, has expressed it more forcibly:

> There is hope of the conversion of a nation of unbelievers; of the conversion of a nation of hyprocrites none. Sincerity in error is respectable; insincerity in the truth is of all things the most reprehensible, for it proves the heart is wholly false, a mass of corruption, in which even divine grace can find, I was about to say, nothing to work upon, certainly nothing likely to concur with it.[4]

As a social reformer he pleaded for peace among the classes. With penetrating analysis he perceived the problems inherent in an industrial society. He worked to ameliorate the lot of the workingman at a time when society understood little of his problems and anxieties. In championing the cause of the workingman against the evils of industrial capitalism, Brownson may have overstated his case, as he so frequently did; but he had to convince Americans of a truth—and so vigorously did he present it that he was labeled a radical. But the reforms that the labor movement has achieved since the Industrial Revolution—many of which are deemed essential today for a well-ordered and free democratic society—show Brownson to have been more of a revolutionary cry in the wilderness than the extremist he appeared one-hundred years ago. Yet, perceiving the dangerous tendencies of his own radical views, he did not hesitate to qualify them in later years. "In my youth I was a wild radical, and sympathized with rebels wherever I found them," he was to write.[5] He then condemned socialism as the panacea to the evils of industrial capitalism. He urged freedom for all classes of society, even for the worker to be free to become a capitalist. His love for religious truth, furthermore, lay at the foundation of his love of truth in the socio-economic order. The moral reform of society, he preached, must be preceded by moral reform in the individuals and in the classes that comprise the components of society.

Brownson's love for truth could not be compromised by coreligionists or sectional considerations. He censured Nativists for their close-minded bigotry and the immigrant Catholics for their foreign loyalties. The truth for him lay in a *via media,* at first unacceptable to either group; and, therefore, it left him without sympathies from either side of the controversy. But again he sacrificed popularity for steadfastness to principle.

Nor was Brownson to enjoy an easy lot in espousing the Southern cause in the North at the beginning of the Civil War. But the dictates of his conscience saw two sides of a complicated controversy, and he was as forceful in condemning the evils of slavery as he was in his too impetuous solution of a long-standing socio-economic problem. He did shift allegiance to the North when war threatened the very life of a nation, as a higher truth had now entered the question; that truth took precedence.

In the field of political philosophy Brownson was equally vigorous in adhering to his principles. No political party could claim his blind allegiance. He became caught in the web of controversial political issues as an American and a Roman Catholic, and he would not compromise the truth as he saw it in order to diminish the opposition to his views. When subsequent thinking and experience convinced him of a modification of his thought, then only would he offer a revision, as he did in the States' rights controversy and in the conflict between the powers of the temporal and the spiritual. But neither political nor social pressure could change the mind of this undaunted lover of truth. Only a conviction, independently arrived at, could alter his stand.

Brownson, the literary critic, judged an author primarily on the basis of his quest for truth. His comments may not have been the kindest, but his analyses were always most penetrating. He longed for a truly American literature, and he looked unsympathetically upon American writers too dependent on European style and thought.

If Brownson so loved truth, why did his tireless energy in its pursuit not win him more followers? Schlesinger has answered this question: "The lonely pursuit for truth, with its worship of unflinching honesty and rigorous logic, was the secret of his failure. While the quest for goodness might have united him to his fellows and given him power to move them, the quest for truth only led to bleak isolation."[6] Brownson stood alone in seeking truth as he was too independent to discuss opposing views with others who also nurtured the same love for truth.

One of the reasons that Brownson could not attract more followers in his time was his too frequent change of views, especially in religious matters. A contributing factor often overlooked is that he was a self-made scholar: he lacked the benefit of mature minds to guide him in his formative years. Without a formal education his thinking evolved from personal experience and readings. Henry Brownson, however, in commenting on his father's self-education, questioned whether a formal education could possibly have benefited such an independent mind: "The strict discipline of the college or university would have filled up some gaps in Brownson's education, but would most likely have made him a routinist and done as much harm as good."[7] Nor could Brownson claim a cultural and urbane environment in his formative years as a compensation for the lack of a formal education. Brought up in the rusticity of a farming community in northern Vermont, he was deprived of a cultural climate so influential for the interchanging of ideas. Nevertheless, it is unfortunate that he put down in writing so many ideas as a young man, which later experience and thought led him to modify. Being dubbed a "weathercock" because of his changing views lessened the influence of his writings.

Unquestionably, Brownson's concept of the truth changed periodically. James Freeman Clarke has portrayed the swinging pendulum of Brownson's thinking in convincing fashion:

He has made the most elaborate and plausible plea for eclecticism, and the most elaborate and plausible plea against it. He has said the best things in favor of transcendentalism, and the best things against it. He has shown that no man can possibly be a Christian, except he is a transcendentalist; and he has also proved that every transcendentalist, whether he knows it or not, is necessarily an infidel. He has satisfactorily shown the truth of socialism, and its necessity in order to bring about a golden age, and he has, by the most convincing arguments, demonstrated that the whole system of socialism is from the pit, and can lead to nothing but anarchy and ruin. . . . He labors now with great ingenuity and extraordinary subtilty to show that there must be an infallible church with its infallible ministry, and that out of this church there can be no salvation. But formerly he labored with equal earnestness to show that there could be no such thing as a church at all, no outward priesthood or ministry.[8]

Yet, as one studies Brownson the searcher for religious truth, the social reformer, and the political philosopher in the context in which his views changed, a logic or continuity of thought is noticed. It is not without reason that he abandons a position or a cause. Condemnation is owed to him who perseveres in what he considers untenable, but admiration is rendered to him who changes a point of view on the basis of new evidence in thinking or from experience. The search for truth is a mental struggle, a Hegelian dialectic *par excellence,* in which the mind, in its active and energetic working upon the ideas it receives, contrasts, distinguishes, analyzes them before it can arrive at a satisfactory, acceptable synthesis that affords mental rest.

As an infant learns to walk by faltering steps, so the searcher for truth must through doubt and tentative hypotheses gradually arrive at a stable position for his mind to hold. Through reading, experience, changing circumstances, and thinking, Brownson found reason to question previous positions. For this he is not to be condemned but praised. An intellectually honest man changes his opinions when new facts require it; he does not hesitate to admit he was wrong. Schlesinger accuses Brownson of not possessing humility; but it requires humility to reject views previously held and for which one fought. Brownson's humility may not have been that of the saint, seasoned with charity and forbearance; but it was the humility of an intellect devoted to truth and impatient with error in others and in itself.

With straightforwardness Brownson could evaluate himself: "Such at least are the conclusions which I have been forced in my own mind to adopt, and such, it seems to me, all must adopt who study the question in the light of Christian theology. I am at least honest in these conclusions, and though I may err now, as I have so often erred before, yet I am not more likely to err than others."[9]

When convinced of error in his own thinking, he admitted the need to correct it: "We may have erred in judgment: when we are shown or are convinced that we have, we shall confess, and make reparation. The best thing is never to err, and the next best thing is to own and correct the error. We claim not the former, but we shall never shrink from the latter."[10]

For all his intellectual honesty and incessant pursuit of truth, Brownson does not enjoy a place of honor in American letters and thought. With the exception of a few Catholic anthologies on American literature, the only mention he receives in textbooks is that of a prominent nineteenth-century controversialist; none of his writings is included for the student to become acquainted with the ideas he advanced. The words of J. H. Allen, although written sixty years ago, were prophetic: "The strong, stormful, rude, yet tenderhearted man passed away, leaving hardly a ripple in our memory to remind us of what his influence had been."[11]

But whatever the popular opinion may have been of Brownson and his ideas in the past, a study by minds free of the heated passions that characterized those of his day can now view them and their author with greater calmness and in broader perspective; for history has shown that Brownson was not a child of his times but was in many ways ahead of his era. Studying Brownson today may well lead many to agree with Russell Kirk that he was "a political philosopher of a high order, a religious essayist of brilliance, a literary critic of force and discernment, a serious journalist at least equal to Lowell and Godkin and Bryant, and one of the shrewdest observers of American character and institutions we ever have been blessed with."[12]

To render Brownson a higher rank in American letters and thought means not necessarily to share his convictions and beliefs. Minds may differ in views without losing respect for each other's judgment and intellectual honesty. To see Brownson as a lover of truth does not require that we accept the truth as he saw it, but it does acknowledge the sincerity and the greatness of an American journalist. Few may become converts to any of Brownson's views; but, whether or not he has convinced us, we may well agree with a writer who was not convinced by Brownson's thought but who wrote:

> Few American readers need to be told who or what is O. A. Brownson. Perhaps no man in this country has, by the simple effort of the pen, made himself more conspicuous, or has more distinctly impressed the peculiarities of his mind. Other writers may have a larger number of readers, but no one has readers of

such various character. He has the attention of intelligent men of
all sects and parties—men who read him without particular regard to the themes on which he spends his energies, or the
sectarian or partisan position of which he may avow himself the
champion. The extraordinary ingenuity of his logic, the vigor
of his thought, and the clearness and directness of his style, will
attract attention, regardless of the particular opinions which
prove the occasion of bringing out these fascinating qualities.[13]

Notes and References

1. Theodore Maynard, *The Story of American Catholicism* (New York, 1948), p. 580.
2. Quoted from Russell Kirk, *Orestes Brownson: Selected Essays* (Chicago, 1955), p. 1.
3. Van Wyck Brooks, *The Flowering of New England* (New York, 1936), pp. 250-51.
4. Arthur M. Schlesinger, Jr., *Orestes A. Brownson* (Boston, 1939), p. 297.
5. Russell Kirk, *The Conservative Mind* (Chicago, 1953), p. 272.

Chapter One

1. Stephen Simpson, "The Working Man's Manual: A New Theory of Political Economy, on the Principle of Production the Source of Wealth," quoted from Joseph Blau, ed., *Social Theories of Jacksonian Democracy* (New York, 1947), pp. 141-42.
2. Leland D. Baldwin, *The Stream of American History* (New York, 1952), p. 613.
3. Quoted from Lindsay Swift, *Brook Farm, Its Members, Scholars, and Visitors* (New York, 1900), p. 15.
4. For a more detailed treatment, see Alice F. Tyler, *Freedom's Ferment* (Minneapolis, 1944), pp. 166-95.
5. New York *Evening Post*, August 6, 1835.
6. New York *Working Men's Advocate*, May 8, 1830.
7. *Farmers', Mechanics', and Workingmen's Advocate*, August 21, 1830.
8. Henry F. Brownson, comp., *The Convert, The Works of Orestes A. Brownson* (Detroit, 1882-87), V, 4.
9. *Ibid.*, p. 7.
10. *Ibid.*, p. 10.
11. *Ibid.*
12. *Ibid.*, p. 18.
13. *Ibid.*, pp. 11-14.
14. Henry F. Brownson, *Orestes A. Brownson's Early Life* (Detroit, 1899), pp. 11-14.
15. *The Convert, Works,* V, 16.
16. *Ibid.*, pp. 32-34.

17. *Ibid.*, p. 37.
18. *Ibid.*, pp. 43-44.
19. *Ibid.*, p. 48.
20. *The Philanthropist*, II, 113.
21. "Charles Elwood," *Works*, IV, 173.
22. *Ibid.*, p. 176.
23. *Ibid.*, p. 185.
24. *Ibid.*, p. 191.
25. *Ibid.*, p. 205.
26. *Ibid.*, p. 223.
27. *Ibid.*, p. 227.
28. *Ibid.*, pp. 231-32.
29. *Ibid.*, pp. 291-92.
30. "Charles Elwood Reviewed," *Works*, IV, 316-61.
31. *Ibid.*, p. 319.
32. *Ibid.*, pp. 333-39.
33. See next chapter.
34. *The Convert, Works*, V, 65-66.
35. *The Philanthropist*, II, 86.
36. "New Views of Christianity, Society, and the Church," *Works*, IV, 4-10.
37. *Ibid.*, pp. 10-14.
38. *Ibid.*, p. 14.
39. *Ibid.*, pp. 14-24.
40. *Ibid.*, p. 26.
41. *Ibid.*, p. 33.
42. *Ibid.*, p. 47.
43. *Ibid.*, p. 55.
44. "Church of the Future," *Works*, IV, 57-58. See also *Works*, V, 83-89.
45. "The Mediatorial Life of Jesus," *Works*, IV, 143.
46. "Leroux on Humanity," *Works*, IV, 100.
47. "The Mediatorial Life of Jesus," *Works*, IV, 138.
48. *Ibid.*, p. 139.
49. John 3:16.
50. "The Mediatorial Life of Jesus," *Works*, IV, 151.
51. Romans 5:19.
52. John, 14:6.
53. "The Mediatorial Life of Jesus," *Works*, IV, 171.
54. Channing to Brownson, June 10, 1842, in H. F. Brownson, *Early Life*, pp. 443-44.
55. Emerson to Elizabeth Peabody, in Ralph L. Lusk, ed., *Emerson's Letters* (New York, 1911), pp. 63-64.

56. "The Mediatorial Life of Jesus," *Works*, IV, 170.

57. *Democratic Review* (November, 1842).

58. For Brownson and Transcendentalism, see Alvan S. Ryan, "The Critique of Transcendentalism," in Harold C. Gardiner, ed., *American Classics Reconsidered* (New York, 1958), pp. 98-120. In three articles of his *Quarterly Review* for 1845 and 1846, Brownson gives a detailed critique of Transcendentalism. He rejects Transcendentalism because it makes man the measure of truth and goodness and since Transcendentalism recognizes no religion as having a supernatural origin. See *Works*, VI, 1-113.

59. For a more complete treatment of Brownson at Brook Farm, see Theodore Maynard, *Orestes Brownson* (New York, 1943), pp. 100-22.

60. *The Convert, Works*, V, 160.

61. *Ibid.*, p. 164.

62. *Ibid.*

63. *Ibid.*, p. 157.

64. *Ibid.*, p. 158.

65. *Ibid.*, p. 159.

66. *Ibid.*, p. 162.

67. *Ibid.*, p. 188. For a more detailed analysis of Brownson's arguments for accepting the divine authority of the Roman Catholic Church, see "The Church Against No-Church," *Works*, V, 331-89; "Faith Not Possible Without the Church," *Works*, V, 417-56; and "The Church a Historical Fact," *Works*, V, 457-75.

68. *The Convert, Works*, V, 185-86.

69. *Brownson's Quarterly Review*, Vol. II, New Series (1848), p. 136.

70. Brownson to J. W. Cummings, June 23, 1849, in H. F. Brownson, *Middle Life*, p. 195.

71. "The Christian Register's Objections," *Works*, VII, 233.

72. Brownson to Montalbert, December 25, 1855, in H. F. Brownson, *Latter Life*, p. 31.

73. Brownson to Hughes, September 1, 1856, in *ibid.*, p. 73.

74. "Archbishop Hughes," *Works*, XIV, 492.

75. "Lacordaire and Catholic Progress," *Works*, XX, 253.

76. "The Existence of God," *Works*, I, 253-75; "Vincenzo Gioberti," *Works*, II, 101-270; and "Ontologism and Psychologism," *Works*, II, 468-86.

77. See Thomas T. McAvoy, "Brownson's Ontologism," *Catholic Historical Review*, XXVIII (1942), 376-81; wherein is contained a letter of Father Henry S. McMurdie of Mt. St. Mary's College, Md., which compares Brownson's philosophical views with the Decrees of

Rome condemning ontologism and Brownson's reply which clarifies his stand and considers himself free from the condemned ontologism.

78. An attempt to absolve Brownson from charges of ontologism is made by Sidney A. Raemers, *America's Foremost Philosopher* (Washington, 1931).

79. *The Spirit-Rapper; An Autobiography, Works,* IX, 1.

80. Maynard, *Brownson,* pp. 223, 227.

81. "The Native Americans," *Works,* XVIII, 286.

82. This reaction was not, however, without some justification. For Brownson had previously remarked in a letter, "Nobody can deny that in external decorum and the ordinary moral and social virtues the Irish Catholics are the most deficient class of our community." See Brownson to J. A. McMaster, March 14, 1849, Brownson Papers, University of Notre Dame Library.

83. Brownson to F. X. Weniger, September 5, 1854, in H. F. Brownson, *Middle Life,* pp. 579-80.

84. Mesmerism is named after Friedrich Anton Mesmer (1733-1815), a German physician, who is supposed to have successfully treated his patients by such a method.

85. *The Spirit-Rapper, Works,* IX, 18-19.

86. *Ibid.,* p. 65.

87. *Ibid.,* p. 77. Earlier in the novel Brownson defined this type of philanthropy as "substituting the love of mankind for the love of God." See pp. 52-53.

88. Schlesinger classifies the book as a work of few merits. See *Brownson,* p. 225; and Maynard sees it as a work of "labored jocularity" and failing in its polemic object. See *Brownson,* pp. 225-26.

89. J. F. Clarke, "Orestes A. Brownson's Argument for the Roman Catholic Church," *Christian Examiner,* XLVIII (1850), 228.

90. John Weiss, *Life and Correspondence of Theodore Parker* (New York, 1864), II, 28.

91. Since *The Convert* has been considered along with the other writings of the author in the presentation of his theological development, an analysis of it is not required. Any study of Brownson, however, would be inadequate without reading it, as the hopes and aspirations, the main events of his life up to his conversion to Roman Catholicism, the authors that have influenced him—all are contained in this autobiography.

92. *The Biblical Repertory and Princeton Review,* (January, 1858), p. 118. Brownson answered this critique of his religious autobiography in "The Princeton Review and the Convert," *Works,* V, 206-40.

93. New York *Herald,* October 8, 1961.

94. "Science and the Sciences," *Works,* IX, 255.

95. *Ibid.,* p. 265.

96. "Faith and the Sciences," *Works,* IX, 270.

97. "Professor Draper's Books," *Works,* IX, 292-318.

98. "The Conflict of Science and Religion," *Works,* IX, 560.

99. "Essays Theological, Philosophical, and Historical on the Reformation in the Sixteenth Century," *Works,* XII, 514-607.

100. H. F. Brownson, *Latter Life,* pp. 449-51.

101. "Essays on the Reformation," *Works,* XII, 581.

102. *Ibid.,* p. 566.

103. See the chapters on the socio-economic and political views of Brownson.

104. See H. F. Brownson, *Latter Life,* pp. 538-43.

105. "Introduction to the Last Series," *Works,* XX, 382.

106. "Here lies Orestes A. Brownson, who humbly acknowledged the true faith, lived a full life, and by writing and speaking bravely defended his Church and country, and granted that his body may have been taken by death, the labors of his mind remain immortal monuments of genius" (translation mine).

Chapter Two

1. *The Convert, Works,* V, 50-57.

2. O. A. Brownson, *An Address on the Fifty-Fifth Anniversary of American Independence Delivered at Ovid, Seneca County, New York* (Ithaca, 1831), pp. 8, 11.

3. H. F. Brownson, *Early Life,* pp. 96-97.

4. Harriet Martineau, *Society in America* (London, 1837), II, 405, 412.

5. *Ibid.,* pp. 357-58.

6. This work has been analyzed in the first chapter.

7. Martineau, *Society in America,* II, 358.

8. "Education of the People," *Christian Examiner,* II (1836), 160.

9. "Tendency of Modern Civilization," *Boston Quarterly Review,* I (1838), 237.

10. "Democracy and Reform," *Boston Quarterly Review,* II (1839), 508.

11. "Democracy of Christianity," *Boston Quarterly Review,* I (1838), 444-73.

12. "Education of the People," *Boston Quarterly Review,* II (1839), 405.

13. "Democracy and Reform," *Boston Quarterly Review,* II (1839), 485.

14. Brownson to MacKenzie, April 22, 1840, in W. L. MacKenzie, *The Life and Times of Martin Van Buren* (Boston, 1846), p. 143.

15. "The Laboring Classes," *Boston Quarterly Review*, III (1840), 370.

16. *Ibid.*

17. *Ibid.*, pp. 394-95.

18. Schlesinger, *Brownson*, p. 99.

19. *Ibid.*, p. 100. Brownson was not the only American who expressed such views. The agrarian Thomas Skidmore advocated the equal division of property among all.

20. H. S. Foxwell in Anton Menger, *The Right to the Whole Produce of Labour* (London, 1899), pp. lxxxix-xc.

21. See Schlesinger, *Brownson*, pp. 101-6.

22. "The Laboring Classes" (second article), *Boston Quarterly Review*, III (1840), 420-512.

23. "Our Future Policy," *Boston Quarterly Review*, IV (1841), 94.

24. "Leroux on Humanity," *Works*, IV, 106-7.

25. "The Mediatorial Life of Jesus," *Works*, IV, 140-72.

26. R. Kirk, *Orestes Brownson: Selected Essays* (Chicago, 1955), p. 11.

27. "The Present State of Society," *Works*, IV, 431.

28. *Ibid.*, p. 433.

29. *Ibid.*, p. 438.

30. *Ibid.*, pp. 439-42.

31. *Ibid.*, pp. 442-44.

32. *Ibid.*, pp. 444-48.

33. *Ibid.*, pp. 448-49.

34. *Ibid.*, p. 450.

35. *Ibid.*

36. *Ibid.*, p. 455.

37. *Ibid.*, p. 459.

38. "Origin and Ground of Government," *Works*, XIII, 364.

39. "The Protective Policy," *Works*, XV, 407.

40. "Origin and Constitution of Government," *Works*, XV, 425.

41. "Come-outerism: or the Radical Tendency of the Day," *Works*, IV, 542.

42. "The Present State of Society," *Works*, IV, 452-53.

43. Schlesinger, *Brownson*, p. 164.

44. "Church Unity and Social Amelioration," *Works*, IV, 512-26. For another article on Fourierism, see "Social Evils, and Their Remedy," *Boston Quarterly Review*, IV (1841), 265-91.

45. *Address on Social Reform* (delivered before the Society of the

Mystical Seven at Wesleyan University, Middletown, Conn., August
7, 1844), p. 9.

46. "No Church, No Reform," *Works*, IV, 511.

47. "Sick Calls," *Works*, X, 595.

48. "Saint-Bonnet on Social Restoration," *Works*, XIV, 235.

49. "Conversations of an Old Man," *Works*, X, 281.

50. *Ibid.*, p. 280.

51. *Ibid.*, p. 279. Brownson also describes his switch to conservatism in "Come-outerism," *Works*, IV, 556-57.

52. "Socialism and the Church," *Works*, X, 80.

53. *Ibid.*, p. 96.

54. *Ibid.*

55. *Ibid.*, p. 97.

56. Boston *Recorder*, September 16, 1825.

57. See *Annual Report of the Boston Society for the Religious and
Moral Instruction of the Poor*, IX (1825), 10; X (1826), 14, 19;
XI (1827), 6, 14-16; XII (1828), 15; *Annual Report of the American Bible Society*, VII (1823), 85-87; X (1826), 85; XII (1828),
70-72.

58. Rev. Lyman Beecher, *Resources of the Adversary and Means
of Their Destruction: a Sermon Preached October 12, 1827, before
the American Board of Missions at New York* (New York, 1827),
p. 13.

59. R. A. Billington, *The Protestant Crusade, 1800-1860: a Study
of the Origins of American Nativism* (New York, 1938), p. 68.

60. "Native Americanism," *Works*, X, 33.

61. "The Native Americans," *Works*, XVIII, 281-300.

62. "The Know-Nothings," *Works*, XVIII, 300-80.

63. *Ibid.*, p. 300.

64. *Ibid.*, p. 301.

65. "Public and Parochial Schools," *Works*, XII, 200-14; "Catholic
Schools and Education," *Works*, XII, 496-514.

66. "Catholic Schools and Education," *Works*, XII, 511.

67. See F. X. Curran, *The Churches and the Schools* (Chicago,
1954); and Sister M. Laurina Kaiser, *Anti-Catholic Attitudes Re-
flected in Elementary History and Geography Textbooks from 1800
to 1850* (Washington, 1953).

68. "Catholic Schools and Education," *Works*, XII, 504.

69. "Slavery—Abolitionism," *Boston Quarterly Review*, I (1838),
240.

70. *Ibid.*

71. "Abolition Proceedings," *Boston Quarterly Review*, I (1838),
500.

72. "The Laboring Classes," *Boston Quarterly Review,* III (1840), 370.

73. "Liberal Studies," *Works,* XIX, 432-33.

74. "Our Future Policy," *Boston Quarterly Review,* IV (1841), 89.

75. "Slavery and the Mexican War," *Works,* XVI, 27.

76. *Ibid.,* pp. 27-28.

77. *Ibid.,* p. 47. See also "Slavery and the Incoming Administration," *Works,* XVII, 60.

78. "Slavery and the Incoming Administration," *Works,* XVII, 54-56.

79. "Emancipation and Colonization," *Works,* XVII, 258.

80. "Slavery and the Church," *Works,* XVII, 317-52.

81. "Liberalism and Progress," *Works,* XX, 345-46.

82. *Ibid.*

83. J. R. Hassard, *The Life of the Most Reverend John Hughes, D.D.* (New York, 1866), p. 437.

84. "Archbishop Hughes on Slavery," *Works,* XVII, 179-210.

85. *Ibid.,* p. 200.

86. "Slavery and the War," *Works,* XVII, 144-78.

87. Brownson to Sumner, December 26, 1862, *Sumner Papers,* Harvard University Library.

88. "The Seward Policy," *Works,* XVII, 356.

89. See H. F. Brownson, *Latter Life,* pp. 402, 404.

90. *Ibid.,* p. 450.

Chapter Three

1. *The Convert, Works,* V, 65-66.

2. *Ibid.,* p. 65.

3. See previous chapter.

4. "The Democratic Principle," *Works,* XVIII, 224. The term "democracy" as used by Brownson here is not to be confused with the commonly accepted view of democracy as a constitutional republic. See also *The Convert, Works,* V, 20-21.

5. *Ibid.,* p. 225.

6. *The Convert, Works,* V, 121.

7. "Constitutional Government," *Works,* XV, 238.

8. This view is shared by H. F. Brownson, "Editor's Preface," *Works,* XV, iii-v, and by L. Roemer, *Brownson on Democracy and the Trend toward Socialism* (New York, 1953), pp. 12-13.

9. "Democracy," *Works,* XV, 4.

10. *Ibid.,* p. 5.

11. *Ibid.,* p. 9.

12. H. F. Brownson, *Early Life,* p. 182.

13. "Democracy," *Works*, XV, 18.
14. *Ibid.*, p. 23.
15. *Ibid.*
16. *Ibid.*, p. 28.
17. Schlesinger, *Brownson*, p. 76.
18. Brownson describes the influence of his readings in the formulation of a reconstructed political philosophy: "I read for the first time Aristotle on Politics; I read the best treatises, ancient and modern, on government within my reach; I studied the constitutions of Greece and Rome, and their history, the political administration of ancient Persia, the feudal system, and the constitutions of modern states, in the light of such experience and such philosophy as I had, and come to the conclusion that the condition of liberty is order, and that in this world we must seek, not equality, but justice. To the maintenance of order in the state, and justice between man and man, a firm, strong, and efficient government is necessary. Liberty is not in the absence of authority, but in being held to obey only just and legitimate authority. Evidently, I had changed systems, and had entered another order of ideas. Government was no longer the mere agent of society, as my democratic masters had taught me, but an authority having the right and the power to govern society, and direct and aid, as a wise providence, in fulfilling its destiny. I became henceforth a conservative in politics, instead of an impracticable radical, and through political conservatism I advanced rapidly towards religious conservatism. So I date my beginning to amend, from the publication of my so-called "horrible doctrines" (*The Convert, Works*, V, 121-22).
19. "Constitutional Government," *Works*, XV, 233.
20. *Ibid.*, p. 238.
21. *Ibid.*, pp. 242-43.
22. Calhoun to Brownson, December 30, 1839, in H. F. Brownson, *Early Life*, pp. 321-22.
23. "Popular Government," *Works*, XV, 293-94.
24. "Slavery—Abolitionism," *Works*, XV, 60.
25. *Ibid.*, pp. 45-63.
26. "Democracy and Liberty," *Works*, XV, 258-59.
27. *Ibid.*, p. 275.
28. *Ibid.*, p. 280.
29. *Ibid.*, pp. 280, 281.
30. "Origin and Ground of Government," *Works*, XV, 297.
31. *Ibid.*, p. 307.
32. *Ibid.*, p. 308.
33. *Ibid.*, p. 347.

34. *Ibid.*, p. 360.
35. *Ibid.*, p. 361.
36. *Ibid.*, pp. 375-76.
37. *Ibid.*, p. 364.
38. *Ibid.*, pp. 363-64.
39. *Ibid.*, p. 364.
40. *Democratic Review*, XIII (1843), 129, 262.
41. Calhoun to Brownson, October 31, 1841, in H. F. Brownson, *Early Life*, p. 305.
42. Isaac Hecker to Brownson, September 14, 1843, in H. F. Brownson, *Early Life*, pp. 340-41.
43. "Origin and Constitution of Government," *Works*, XV, 424.
44. "Calhoun's Life and Speeches," *Works*, XV, 456.
45. *Ibid.*, p. 468.
46. "Mr. Calhoun and the Baltimore Convention," *Works*, XV, 473-83.
47. "The Presidential Nominations," *Works*, XV, 484-85.
48. *Ibid.*, p. 485.
49. "The Recent Election," *Works*, XV, 519.
50. "The Protective Policy," *Works*, XV, 493-507.
51. "The Recent Election," *Works*, XV, 519-20.
52. "National Greatness," *Works*, XV, 523-45.
53. *Ibid.*, p. 533.
54. "Political Constitutions," *Works*, XV, 556.
55. *Ibid.*, p. 566.
56. "Conversations of an Old Man and His Young Friends," *Works*, X, 281.
57. H. F. Brownson, *Middle Life*, p. 419.
58. *Ibid.*, pp. 423-24.
59. *Ibid.*, pp. 455-68.
60. *Ibid.*, p. 469.
61. "Christian Politics," *Works*, XII, 345.
62. "Temporal and Spiritual," *Works*, XI, 15-16.
63. *Ibid.*, p. 22.
64. *Ibid.*
65. "The Spiritual Not for the Temporal," *Works*, XI, 39.
66. *Ibid.*, pp. 36-37.
67. *Ibid.*, pp. 42-44.
68. "The Spiritual Order Supreme," *Works*, XI, 83-89.
69. *Ibid.*, p. 87.
70. H. F. Brownson, *Middle Life*, p. 490.
71. *Ibid.*, p. 494.
72. *Ibid.*, p. 498.

73. *Ibid.*, pp. 592-93.
74. *Ibid.*, pp. 501-2.
75. See preceding chapter.
76. H. F. Brownson, *Middle Life*, pp. 503-9.
77. *Ibid.*, p. 589.
78. *Ibid.*, p. 637.
79. *Ibid.*
80. See Chapter 1.
81. "The Church and the Republic," *Works*, XII, 1-32.
82. *Ibid.*, p. 32.
83. "Brownson on the Church and the Republic," *Works*, XII, 45.
84. "A Response to O. A. Brownson," *Universalist Quarterly Review* (April, 1857); "Christianity as an Organization," *Universalist Quarterly Review* (October, 1857).
85. "Separation of Church and State," *Works*, XII, 409.
86. "Pope and Emperor," *Works*, XII, 444.
87. "Rights of the Temporal," *Works*, XII, 382.
88. *Ibid.*, p. 387.
89. *Ibid.*, p. 385.
90. *Ibid.*, p. 386.
91. *Ibid.*, pp. 389-99, 404.
92. H. F. Brownson, *Latter Life*, pp. 219, 220.
93. *Ibid.*, pp. 236, 237.
94. *Ibid.*, p. 287.
95. *Ibid.*, p. 257.
96. *Ibid.*, pp. 254-55.
97. "The Church Not a Despotism," *Works*, XX, 215.
98. *Ibid.*, pp. 220-21.
99. "Saint-Worship," *Works*, VIII, 146.
100. *Ibid.*
101. "Papal Infallibility," *Works*, XIII, 414-15.
102. "The Struggle of the Nation for Life," *Works*, XVII, 220.
103. *Ibid.*, pp. 221-22.
104. "State Rebellion, State Suicide," *Works*, XVII, 228-53.
105. "The Federal Constitution," *Works*, XVII, 480.
106. "Are the United State A Nation?" *Works*, XVII, 566.
107. "I could not have written my work without the aid derived from its suggestions, any more than I could without Plato, Aristotle, St. Augustine, St. Thomas, Suarez, Pierre Leroux, and the Abbate Gioberti" ("The American Republic," *Works*, XVIII, 3).
108. The best analysis of *The American Republic* has been done by Thomas I. Cook and Armand B. Leavelle, "Orestes A. Brownson's

The American Republic," Review of Politics, IV (1942), 77-93, 173-93.

109. *The Convert, Works,* V, 126.

110. Brownson seemed to be unaware of the cosmopolitanism of the Roman Stoics, who in their teaching of universal brotherhood and equal rights for all men, contributed to the Roman Empire's uniting of the Mediterranean world and the granting of limited privileges of citizenship even to conquered members of the Empire.

111. *The American Republic, Works,* XVIII, 207.

112. *Ibid.,* p. 198.

113. *Ibid.,* p. 209.

114. *Ibid.,* p. 217.

115. *Ibid.,* p. 212.

116. *Ibid.,* p. 217.

117. *Ibid.,* p. 212. These same views are reiterated and expanded upon in "The Papacy and the Republic," *Works,* XIII, 323-51.

118. *Ibid.,* p. 5.

119. L. Roemer differs from this opinion. He considers that *The American Republic* cannot possibly be the best of Brownson's works principally because it shies away from the controversialism of previous political writings. See Roemer, *Brownson,* p. 25.

120. Maynard, *Brownson,* p. 340.

121. Joseph P. Donovan, "Giant Among Giants," *Columbia,* VI (1927), 36.

122. Schlesinger, *Brownson,* p. 261.

123. New York *Tribune,* December 28, 1865.

124. "The Democratic Principle," *Works,* XVIII, 223.

125. *Ibid.,* p. 226.

126. Cook and Leavelle, "*The American Republic,*" p. 191.

127. *Ibid.*

Chapter Four

1. "Wordsworth's Poetical Works," *Works,* XIX, 422.

2. "The Vision of Sir Launfal," *Works,* XIX, 312-13.

3. "Catholicity and Literature," *Works,* XIX, 448.

4. "Dana's Poems and Prose Writings," *Works,* XIX, 317-18.

5. "The Works of Daniel Webster," *Works,* XIX, 363.

6. Schlesinger, *Brownson,* p. 235.

7. "Origin and Ground of Government," *Works,* XV, 299.

8. *Ibid.*

9. "American Literature," *Works,* XIX, 3.

10. A. W. Brown, *William Ellery Channing* (New York, 1961), p. 118.

11. "American Literature," *Works*, XIX, 26.
12. "Literature, Love and Marriage," *Works*, XIX 494.
13. *Ibid.*, p. 505.
14. *Ibid.*, p. 497.
15. "American Literature," *Works*, XIX, 210.
16. *Ibid.*, p. 217.
17. "R. W. Emerson's Poems," *Works*, XIX, 189-202.
18. "Emerson's Prose Works," *Works*, III, 424.
19. *Ibid.*, pp. 424-38. For a study of the fundamental religious and philosophical differences between these two authors, see A. Robert Caponigri, "Brownson and Emerson: Nature and History," *New England Quarterly Review*, XVIII (1945), 368-90.
20. "The Vision of Sir Launfal," *Works*, XIX, 315.
21. *Ibid.*, pp. 308-17.
22. "Beecher's Norwood," *Works*, XIX, 533.
23. *Ibid.*
24. *Ibid.*, p. 541.
25. *Ibid.*, pp. 536, 543.
26. "Dana's Poems and Prose Writings," *Works*, XIX, 317-42.
27. "The Works of Daniel Webster," *Works*, XIX, 343-81.
28. "Bancroft's History of the United States," *Works*, XIX, 382.
29. *Ibid.*, pp. 382-418.
30. *The American Republic, Works*, XVIII, 1.
31. "Cooper's Ways of the Hour," *Works*, XVI, 339-40.
32. *Ibid.*, pp. 340-49.
33. H. F. Brownson, *Middle Life*, pp. 256-57.
34. "The Works of Daniel Webster," *Works*, XIX, 367.
35. "The Woman Question," *Works*, XVIII, 384.
36. "Women's Novels," *Works*, XIX, 598.
37. "Religious Novels," *Works*, XIX, 567.
38. See Thomas R. Ryan's essay "On Women Novelists," in *Sailor's Snug Harbor: Studies in Brownson's Thought* (New York, 1952), pp. 68-79.
39. "The Catholic Press," *Works*, XIX, 280-82.
40. "Catholicity and Literature," *Works*, XIX, 451-52.
41. *Ibid.*, p. 454.
42. "Catholic Secular Literature," *Works*, XIX, 301.
43. "The Literary Policy of the Church of Rome," *Works*, VI, 520-49.
44. "American Literature," *Works*, XIX, 14.
45. *Ibid.*, pp. 14-15.
46. "The Papacy and the Republic," *Works*, XIII, 338.
47. "The Catholic Press," *Works*, XIX, 269.

48. *Ibid.*

49. *Ibid.*, p. 288.

50. Writing of the Roman Catholic religion, Brownson states: "It acknowledges no master but God, and depends only on the divine will in respect to what it shall teach, what it shall ordain, what it shall insist upon as truth, piety, moral and social virtue. It was not made by the people, but for them; is administered not by the people, but for them; is accountable not to the people, but to God. Not dependent on the people, it will not follow their passions; not subject to their control, it will not be their accomplice in iniquity; and speaking from God, it will teach them the truth, and command them to practice justice" ("Catholicity Necessary to Democracy," *Works*, X, 12).

51. "Modern French Literature," *Works*, XIX, 49.

52. *Ibid.*

53. *Ibid.*

54. *Ibid.*, pp. 55-57.

55. *Ibid.*, pp. 53-55.

56. "Catholic Popular Literature," *Works*, XIX, 589-90.

57. "American Literature," *Works*, XIX, 33.

58. "Etudes de Theologie," *Works*, XIX, 472.

59. *Ibid.*, pp. 472-73.

60. "Synthetic Philosophy," *Works*, I, 101.

61. "Religious Novels," *Works*, XIX, 152.

62. See Chapter 2.

63. "The Present State of Society," *Works*, IV, 427.

64. *Ibid.*, p. 426.

65. "Religious Novels," *Works*, XIX, 152.

66. *Ibid.*, pp. 152-53.

67. "Uncle Jack and His Nephews," *Works*, XI, 218.

68. "Wordsworth's Poetical Works," *Works*, XIX, 418-30.

69. "Philosophy and Common Sense," *Works*, I, 4.

70. "The Present State of Society," *Works*, IV, 423.

71. "Carlyle's French Revolution," *Works*, XIX, 44.

72. "The Rationalistic Theory," *Works*, IV, 383.

73. "Philosophy of the Supernatural," *Works*, II, 274.

74. "Cardinal Wiseman's Essays," *Works*, X, 450.

75. *Ibid.*, p. 451.

76. "Newman's Development of Christian Doctrine," *Works*, XIX, 9, 25.

77. *Ibid.*, p. 25.

78. See H. F. Brownson, *Middle Life*, pp. 34-74, 386-97.
79. "Morris on the Incarnation," *Works*, XIV, 175.
80. Maynard, *Brownson*, p. 205.

Chapter Five

1. "Explanations to Catholics," *Works*, XX, 380.
2. I. Hecker, "Dr. Brownson and Catholicity," *Catholic World*, XLVI (1887), 234.
3. Alvan S. Ryan, ed., *The Brownson Reader* (New York, 1955), p. 2.
4. *The Convert, Works*, V, 48.
5. "Conversations of an Old Man," *Works*, X, 279.
6. Schlesinger, *Brownson*, p. 292.
7. H. F. Brownson, *Early Life*, p. 368.
8. J. F. Clarke, "Orestes A. Brownson's Argument for the Roman Church," *Christian Examiner*, XLVIII (1850), 228-29.
9. *The Spirit-Rapper, Works*, XI, 225.
10. "Introduction to National Series," *Brownson's Quarterly Review*, Third New York Series, IV (1863), 128.
11. Joseph H. Allen, *Our Liberal Movement in Theology* (Boston, 1882), p. 88.
12. Kirk, *Brownson*, p. 1.
13. "Brownson on the Church and the Republic," *Universalist Quarterly and General Review.* Quoted from Brownson's *Works*, XII, 33-34.

Selected Bibliography

PRIMARY SOURCES

1. Bibliographies

Incomplete bibliographies of Brownson are contained in *The Guide to Catholic Literature, 1888-1940* (Detroit, 1940), pp. 142-43, and in Robert E. Spiller's *Literary History of the United States* (New York, 1948), III, 421-22 and its Bibliographic Supplement (1959), p. 86.

More thorough bibliographies are contained in Theodore Maynard, *Orestes Brownson: Yankee, Radical, Catholic* (New York, 1943), pp. 433-43; and Arthur M. Schlesinger, Jr., *Orestes Brownson: A Pilgrim's Progress* (Boston, 1939), pp. 299-305.

2. Manuscript Materials

Brownson Papers, University of Notre Dame Archives. This collection consists largely of letters to Brownson, some letters by him, and drafts of his articles.

3. Works by Brownson

Address on Intemperance. Keene, New Hampshire: J. & J. W. Prentiss, 1833.

The American Republic: Its Constitution, Tendencies, and Destiny. New York: P. O'Shea, 1866.

Boston Quarterly Review, Vols. 1-5, 1838-1842.

Brownson's Quarterly Review. Vols. 1-3, 1844-1846. New Series: Vols. 1-6, 1846-1852. Third Series: Vols. 1-3, 1853-1855. New York Series: Vols. 1-4, 1856-1859. Second and Third New York Series: Vols. 1-4, 1860-1863. National Series: Vol. 1, 1864. Last Series: Vols. 1-3, 1873-1875.

Charles Elwood, or The Infidel Converted. Boston: C. C. Little and and J. Brown, 1840.

Conversations on Liberalism and the Church. New York: D. & J. Sadlier, 1870.

The Convert: or Leaves from My Experience. New York: D. & J. Sadlier, 1857.

Essays and Reviews, Chiefly on Theology, Politics, and Socialism. New York: D. & J. Sadlier, 1852.

The Mediatorial Life of Jesus. Boston: C. C. Little and J. Brown, 1842.

Selected Bibliography

New Views of Christianity, Society, and the Church. Boston: C. C. Little and J. Brown, 1836.
The Spirit-Rapper: an Autobiography. Boston: Little, Brown & Co., 1854.

4. *Compilations of Brownson's Works*

The Brownson Reader. Edited by Alvan S. Ryan. New York: P. J. Kennedy, 1955.
Brownson's Works. Edited by Henry F. Brownson. Detroit: Thorndike Nourse, 1882-87. 20 vols. Virtually all of Brownson's writings as a Catholic are herein contained, with most of the important writings that appeared before 1844.
Literary, Scientific, and Political Views of Orestes A. Brownson. Edited by Henry F. Brownson. New York: Benziger, 1893.
Orestes A. Brownson's Early Life: from 1803 to 1844. Edited by Henry F. Brownson. Detroit: H. F. Brownson, 1898.
Orestes A. Brownson's Middle Life: from 1845 to 1855. Edited by Henry F. Brownson. Detroit: H. F. Brownson, 1899.
Orestes A. Brownson's Latter Life: from 1855 to 1876. Edited by Henry F. Brownson. Detroit: H. F. Brownson, 1900. These three volumes contain many documents and correspondence not available in other works; although the material is poorly organized, the books are a necessary and indispensable tool for a study of Brownson.
Orestes Brownson: Selected Essays. Edited by Russell Kirk. Chicago: Henry Regnery Co., 1955.
Watchwords from Dr. Brownson. Edited by D. J. Scannell O'Neill. Techny, Ill.: Society of the Divine Word, 1910.

SECONDARY SOURCES

CAPONIGRI, A. ROBERT. "Brownson and Emerson: Nature and History," *New England Quarterly,* XVIII (1945), 368-90. Study of the philosophical and religious issues that served as a basis for Brownson's criticism of Emerson.
CLARKE, JAMES FREEMAN. "Orestes A. Brownson's Argument for the Catholic Church," *Christian Examiner,* XLVIII (1850), 227-47. Effort to bring out the inconsistencies in the reasons Brownson offered about rejecting Protestantism in favor of Roman Catholicism.
CONROY, PAUL R. "Orestes A. Brownson: American Political Philosopher." Unpublished Ph.D. dissertation (St. Louis University, 1937).

————. "The Role of the American Constitution in the Political Philosophy of Orestes A. Brownson," *Catholic Historical Review,* XXV (1939), 271-86.

COOK, THOMAS I. and LEAVELLE, ARMAND B. "Orestes A. Brownson's *The American Republic,*" *Review of Politics,* IV (1942), 77-93, 173-93. Best analysis and evaluation of Brownson's political thought and of its significance today.

CORRIGAN, SISTER M. FELICIA. *Some Social Principles of Orestes A. Brownson.* Washington: Catholic University of America Press, 1939. Examination of how Brownson's social principles apply to the religious, political, economic, educational orders and to the family.

FARRELL, BERTIN. *Orestes Brownson's Approach to the Problem of God.* Washington: Catholic University of America Press, 1950.

FITZSIMONS, M. A. "Brownson's Search for the Kingdom of God: The Social Thought of an American Radical," *Review of Politics,* XVI (1954), 22-36. Overemphasis on earlier radical years of Brownson and not sufficient study of later, more sobering approach to society.

FRESE, JOSEPH R. "Brownson on Know-Nothingism," *Historical Records and Studies,* XXVIII (1937), 52-74.

GILDEA, WILLIAM L. "An English View of Brownson's Conversion," *Catholic World,* LXIX (1899), 24-31.

GORMAN, ROBERT. *Catholic Apologetical Literature in the United States (1784-1858).* Washington: Catholic University of America Press, 1939. Defense of Catholicism in the United States in the context of American Protestantism.

HOFFMAN, ROSS J. "*The American Republic* and Western Christendom," *Historical Records and Studies,* XXXV (1946), 3-17. Brownson's greatness and limitation in viewing America in its historical and political relations with the rest of the world.

HURLEY, DANIEL A. "Orestes Augustus Brownson's Way to the Catholic Church." Unpublished M.A. dissertation (St. Bonaventure College, 1946).

LADU, ARTHUR I. "Political Ideas of Orestes A. Brownson, Transcendentalist," *Philological Quarterly,* XII (1933), 280-89. Attempt to show that Brownson's political philosophy was a result of his belief in Transcendentalism.

MALONE, GEORGE K. *The True Church: a Study in the Apologetics of Orestes Augustus Brownson.* Mundelein, Ill.: St. Mary of the Lake Seminary, 1957. Study of the various arguments that Brownson employed to prove that the Catholic Church is the only church that Christ established.

MAYNARD, THEODORE. *Orestes Brownson: Yankee, Radical, Catholic.* New York: Macmillan Co., 1943. Full-length biography, especially valuable for his years as a Roman Catholic.

McAVOY, THOMAS T. "Brownson's Ontologism," *Catholic Historical Review,* XXVIII (1942), 376-81. Contains letter of Henry S. McMurdie of Mt. St. Mary's College, Maryland, comparing Brownson's philosophical views with Decrees of Rome condemning ontologism and Brownson's reply which clarifies his stand and considers himself free from the condemned philosophical position.

————. "Orestes A. Brownson and American History," *Catholic Historical Review,* XL (1954), 257-68. Study of Brownson as he reflects the American environment in which he lived and how he sought to give it a new image.

McMAHON, FRANCIS E. "Orestes Brownson on Church and State," *Theological Studies,* XV (1954), 175-228.

MICHEL, VIRGIL G. "Brownson's Political Philosophy and Today," *American Catholic Quarterly Review,* XLIV (1919), 193-202. Discussion of Brownson's political views in the light of subsequent historical events.

————. *The Critical Principles of Orestes A. Brownson.* Washington: Catholic University of America Press, 1918. Attempt to infer from Brownson's own writings a set of critical and esthetic principles by which to judge literature.

PARRY, STANLEY J. "The Premises of Brownson's Political Theory," *Review of Politics,* XVI (1954), 194-211. Study of the metaphysical foundations of Brownson's political thought.

POWER, EDWARD J. "The Educational Views and Attitudes of Orestes A. Brownson." Unpublished Ph.D. dissertation (University of Notre Dame, 1949).

RAEMERS, SIDNEY A. *America's Foremost Philosopher.* Washington: Catholic University of America Press, 1931. Engaging appraisal of Brownson's thought, but position untenable.

REIDL, JOHN. "The Life and Philosophy of Orestes Brownson." Unpublished Ph.D. dissertation (Marquette University, 1930). Traces the influence of the philosophers who influenced Brownson.

ROEMER, LAWRENCE. *Brownson on Democracy and the Trend toward Socialism.* New York: Philosophical Library, 1953. Examination of Brownson's political and social principles, with emphasis on the arguments employed to support his conclusions; shows how Brownson noted the development of trends toward socialism and communism in the nineteenth century.

RYAN, ALVAN S. "Orestes A. Brownson: The Critique of Transcendentalism," in Harold C. Gardiner, *American Classics Reconsidered: A Christian Appraisal.* New York: Charles Scribner's Sons, 1958. Excellent essay on Brownson first as a spokesman for, and subsequently as a forceful critic of, Transcendentalism, pp. 98-120.

RYAN, EDWIN. "Brownson and Newman," *American Ecclesiastical Review,* LII (1915), 406-13. Study of the theological controversy engaged in by these two converts to Roman Catholicism.

SARGENT, DANIEL. *Four Independents.* New York: Sheed & Ward, 1935. Contains an interesting chapter on Brownson, but lacks accuracy.

SCHLESINGER, ARTHUR M., JR. *Orestes Brownson: A Pilgrim's Progress.* Boston: Little, Brown & Co., 1939. Best study of Brownson as a non-Catholic and of his socio-economic views; his Catholic years are incompletely treated, leaving out many facts pertinent to a thorough study of the author.

SHAUGHNESSY, SISTER JEROME. "Dr. Orestes A. Brownson's Philosophy of Nationalism." Unpublished M.A. dissertation (University of Notre Dame, 1926).

SOLETA, CHESTER A. "The Literary Criticism of O. A. Brownson," *Review of Politics,* XVI (1954), 334-51.

STEFUN, BONAVENTURE. "Orestes Brownson: Apologist," *Homiletic and Pastoral Review,* LXIII (1962), 40-47. Explanation of Brownson's rationale for leading non-Catholics to Catholicism.

WHALEN, DORAN. *Granite for God's House.* New York: Sheed & Ward, 1941. Popularly written biography of Brownson but lacks documentation; contains a number of inaccuracies; is partisan.

————. "Some Aspects of the Influence of Orestes A. Brownson on His Contemporaries." Unpublished Ph.D. dissertation (University of Notre Dame, 1933).

Index

Index

Index